YOUR INTUITION LED YOU HERE

YOUR INTUITION LED YOU HERE

Daily Rituals for Empowerment, Inner Knowing, AND Magic

ALEX NARANJO & MARLENE VARGAS

RODALE.
New York

Published in the United States by Rodale Books, an imprint of Random House,
a division of Penguin Random House LLC, New York.
rodalebooks.com

RODALE and the Plant colophon are registered trademarks of Penguin Random House LLC.
Library of Congress Cataloging-in-Publication Data is available upon request.

ISBN 978-0-593-13948-6
Ebook ISBN 978-0-593-13949-3

Printed in the United States of America

Editor: Donna Loffredo
Illustrations: Valentina Zapata
Cover design: Robert Diaz
Book design: Jan Derevjanik
Production Editor: Serena Wang
Production Manager: Heather Williamson
Composition: North Market Street Graphics
Copy Editor: Robin Slutzky
Indexer: Jay Kreider

1st Printing

First Edition

DEDICATION

This book is dedicated to the spirit world—to our ancestors, spirit guides, and God.

CONTENTS

INTRODUCTION

INTRODUCTION

IN CASE YOU HAVEN'T NOTICED, WE ARE LIVING IN A TIME DURING WHICH LIFE CAN sometimes seem less than magical on a day-to-day basis. But that's just on the surface. Look a little closer, and you can probably see that there are plenty of examples of magic at play in your own life, even if you've never performed a single ritual. Call it synchronicity, call it coincidence, call it what you will—but peel back the layers, and most of us have at least caught glimpses of some of the ways in which there seem to be greater powers at play in our life behind the scenes.

Here's the thing: *You* are that power, you just may not have realized it yet. Think about that, then imagine what would happen if you actually acknowledged and tapped into that innate power that you have to create your own life!

Magic and intuition are an integral part of who we are as human beings. In fact, magic has been a part of every culture dating back to the BC era. There's a reason for that—while we tend to think of magic as something outside of ourselves, it's actually a very basic and essential part of being human. It offers us a way of growing, connecting, and coming into our power. It's only recently, as we've become more fixated on science as a society, that the focus on and belief in magic have started to diminish. In some circles, at least. As the founders of the metaphysical shop House of Intuition, belief in magic is alive and well in our circle!

We founded House of Intuition (HOI or, as we like to call it, "hoy") because we felt it was important to provide people with an accessible way of tapping into their own intuitive wisdom. Through this wisdom comes self-empowerment. At the end of the day, that's really what magic is all about to us. This book is an extension of our goal to make that magic accessible to as many people as possible. We want you to personally experience how your own intuition can lead you to all of the best places in life, if only you just learn to trust. Spoiler alert: We are not going to teach you anything in this book that you don't already know on some level. We are simply going to draw your attention to things you may have dismissed or discounted.

If you have a sense that there is something more out there but can't put your finger on exactly what that something is, you've come to the right place. If you're searching for answers and looking for new solutions, we're glad you're here! If you're curious about magic, but don't know where to begin, welcome! If you are open to the idea of new possibilities, we're glad to have you.

Through our own story, we're going to show you what magic looks like in practice. It's simultaneously more subtle and more profound than you might guess. We're going to show you how normal and accessible magic really is. Guaranteed, we are the least "witchy" people you could ever hope to meet and, at one point, we probably would have been voted the Least Likely to Own a Magic Shop. Yet, here we are. We are going to walk you through the process of establishing a magic practice and discuss the same sort of things we talk about with our customers all the time, like "Is magic evil?" and "Where do I start?"

But before we go any further, we should probably clear up a few things that are important to understand about magic and what we mean when we use that word:

1. **Magic isn't what you think it is.**
2. **Magic is powerful—because *you* are powerful.**
3. **There are no perfect answers—it's up to you to find the answers that are right for you, and this book will give you a starting point for doing that.**

And the *most* important thing to understand here is that we are not talking about magic in the pull-a-rabbit-out-of-a-hat sense of the word. To us, magic is about connection. It's about intentionally connecting with the forces bigger than ourselves who are here for the sole purpose of protecting and helping us through this life. But, most of all, magic is about connecting with the power we all hold within—and our intuition is the primary way through which we make that connection. Just like HOI is a metaphysical shop that is ultimately designed to bring people closer to their intuition by allowing them to use it in new ways, so is this book.

We all want a bit of magic in our lives. Every single day, the two of us are reminded how important the idea of magic is to people—whether they want to admit it or not. Clients may be timid when they first step into HOI, but they don't leave that way. We've cried with customers, we've consoled customers, and we've celebrated with customers. We help them find the strength and power within themselves to bring the things that are the most important to them to fruition. This is personal work, and it is also deeply meaningful. Magic (and, specifically, the sense of connection and empowerment it brings) gives us a sense of security and empowerment. It instills in us the belief that we have options to create what we desire. Magic is the small glimmer way over there at the end of the tunnel. The sliver of light that we sometimes desperately need to see in order to keep moving forward.

There are so many different types of magic in this world. There is the practice of magic, which involves things like herbs, oils, and rituals, and that can serve as a tool we can all use as needed. This type of magic works but, in our opinion, it's not long-lasting. The real magic is inside of us. And that's the real purpose of ritualistic magic: The rituals (including the ones we share in this book) will draw you closer to accessing and acknowledging the magic that's already inside of you.

That inner magic wants to rise to the surface and come out to play in all of our lives. The rituals simply provide us with a means to get closer to that magic so that we can listen to and trust ourselves and the universe more easily. Rituals provide a tactile, focused practice that draws our awareness to the fact that we are the powerful creators of our own lives. Rituals require us to direct our attention to an intention and, with that, recognize that: (1) we know what we need—we already have all the answers (hello, intuition!) and (2) when we concentrate on the outcomes we want to manifest, we can bring them to fruition. Magical rituals allow us to align with our true self, as well as with the powerful forces at work in the universe. Rituals provide us with a way of understanding how powerful we really are, especially when we work with the universe.

Feel free to make this book your own and to use it in whatever way you feel called to. You can read it straight through from cover to cover, or you can dip in time and time again to find the specific rituals and information you need at any given moment. Our greatest hope is that, after a while, you don't use this book at all, because you have come to realize that all the magic and answers lie not between the covers of a book, but within you.

PART ONE

OUR STORY

CHAPTER ONE

FROM THE ASHES

MARLENE'S STORY

I WAS BORN WITH THE URGE TO BELONG TO SOMETHING POWERFUL, SOMETHING bigger than myself. Since I was raised in a Catholic family, church was naturally the first place I turned to for spiritual fulfillment and a sense of connection to a higher source. Growing up, I was very much into Catholicism, despite also feeling disconnected from it in a way I couldn't quite put my finger on.

There are so many things we innately know as children but don't have the words to explain. As a kid, I never would have described (or even thought of) myself as having a relationship with the dead (aka spirit), even though I did. I couldn't have told you at the time that I was able to sense the presence of spirits through what I now understand to be mediumship, even though that's exactly what I was doing. Now, listen, I don't mean I was one of those kids who was talking to dead people. But I *did* understand there were presences around me . . . I just couldn't quite figure out what those presences were or how to get to them.

As a very young child, I used to place lit candles on my Barbie case and watch the flame dance and flicker as I said hello to that nebulous presence. My sister was often with me when I did this, and she would get super freaked out every time. I wasn't a gothic little kid or anything like that—I just wanted the spirits that I somehow knew were lurking in the shadows to come out and play with me.

All of this is to say that, from very early on, I was in touch with some sort of greater spiritual force outside the confines of religion. That force was elusive, though, and, with the exception of my freaked-out sister, it felt like a secret for me to keep. It definitely wasn't something I felt like I could talk about with my family. I understood that the things I felt and was interested in flew in the face of their Catholic beliefs.

Looking back, I can see that, like most kids, I came to this earth connected to something greater than myself. Also like most kids, that innate connection and belief were largely snuffed out by well-meaning adults. My intuition was right there chatting away with me all along, but as the years went by I was conditioned to disconnect from it. It's unfortunate, because it's so much easier to nurture our inborn intuition than it is to either shut that intuition down altogether and live a disconnected life, or to go through the process of rediscovering our intuitive nature as an adult.

Over time, I moved away from my secret little spiritual practices and joined the rest of my family in a more traditional religious life. At first that meant Catholicism, but over time I was turned off by some of the practices. Specifically, I felt uncomfortable with mandatory confessions. I didn't understand the point of confessing my sins to a man in a box, or how a prescribed set of seemingly arbitrary prayers would absolve me. At my sister's wedding, I finally put my foot down and refused to partake in confession, as the wedding party was obligated to do. As a result, I was refused communion during the ceremony, despite the fact that I was a baptized, confirmed, practicing Catholic. It made no sense to me.

When I turned eighteen, I turned toward nondenominational Christianity, primarily because the priests felt more approachable and it didn't require confessionals. In my typical way, once I was in, I went hard. I went to Bible school, was baptized into the church, attended three times a week, and felt it was my mission to get everyone else to come along with me. I was that person you see at the gym, reading the Gospel while speed walking. I spoke the Word to anyone and everyone who would listen, and sometimes to those who didn't want to listen, too. I was all good with nondenominational Christianity until I was told that I had to bring my Catholic parents into the church because, if I didn't, they were doomed to eternal damnation. "Oh, *hell* no," I thought. I stopped going to church, and started to feel spiritually lost once again. I craved something more, but since I couldn't put my finger on exactly what that something more was, I had no idea how to find it.

In my twenties, I had my son, Eric. When I broke up with his father a few years later, I fell in love with a woman and we got married and raised my son together. Even though I was no longer an active member of either church, it was still important to me that Eric have a spiritual foundation like I'd had as a child. Plus, I still carried with me some of the beliefs and practices of each of those religions and continued to feel a connection to them. So I sent Eric to a Christian school. Everything was good until the day Eric was told that he couldn't watch Disney movies because Disney gave gay people insurance, and gay people were damned to go to hell. As a gay woman, I couldn't have my son going to a school that told him the love that laid the foundation of his home and life was not only wrong, but downright evil.

Religion continued to be an ongoing conundrum in my life, an area that was filled with question marks and a sense of longing that buzzed in the background. But, in the meantime, life went on. In fact, things seemed to be going pretty well. By the time I reached my early thirties, I was what I considered to be successful, which was important to me. I owned a medical billing company that my sister helped me run, and had also invested in several real estate properties. My family struggled financially when I was growing up, and I wanted Eric to have a different experience. As each year passed, I fell deeper and deeper into the material world and the daily grind that came with it. My life was all about raising Eric, focusing on my business, and accumulating wealth.

Then came 2007. Oh, 2007.

Everyone talks about the Great Recession of 2008, but as any investor will tell you, it was in 2007 that the real estate market started its downward slide. Like so many others, I did not fare well. My tenants stopped paying their rent because they lost their jobs. This was bad news because I didn't have the type of reserves I needed on hand to save my investment properties. Everything went belly up. It was hard, but I knew that my family was going to be okay because the medical billing company wasn't impacted by the crash. Plus, my wife was an RN, so she made a good income that continued to support our family. Times weren't easy and I didn't like what was happening, but we were getting it done. We were okay.

A little more than three weeks before my birthday that year, I got a phone call that changed everything. As I was sitting around a table having dinner with clients, I got a call that my aunt Ruthie—who was like a mother to me, and one of the most important guiding forces in my life—had been admitted to the ER for stomach pain. As soon as I heard the news, I knew it wasn't good. Way deep down in my gut, I knew this was the end for Aunt Ruthie. I stood up, left the restaurant, and drove from Bakersfield straight to the ER in Torrance. There I learned that Aunt Ruthie had pancreatic cancer and that the doctors couldn't do anything about it. I spent the next seventeen days right there by my aunt's side. She passed the day after my birthday. Never before have I been taken to my knees like I was by losing Aunt Ruthie.

Of course, life went on, and I continued to go through the motions, despite the overwhelming pain and grief I felt. I continued to run the medical billing company with my sister, who also lived with her kids in the front unit of the duplex my wife and I owned. My sister had recently broken up with her husband and, like many people going through a divorce, she just wanted to go out and have fun. I've always been more of a homebody, but my wife liked to go out, so I encouraged her to keep my sister company.

One night shortly after Aunt Ruthie died, I woke up in the middle of the night and strongly felt her presence in the room. In that moment, everything felt clear; I didn't question what was happening. I couldn't see Aunt Ruthie, but I distinctly felt her pulling me up out of bed until I was standing in the middle of the room. There, I looked around and noticed that my wife wasn't in bed. Strange. She had gone out with my sister earlier that evening, but now it was three o'clock in the morning. I walked over to the window and looked out to see if my sister's car was in the driveway. It was. "Oh, good. They're home," I thought. I walked downstairs and opened the back door so that I could walk to the front unit and make sure my wife was there with her.

I tried to open my sister's door, only to find that it was locked. Normally, I would have knocked, but I heard my aunt's voice in my ear, clear as day. "Go get your keys," she said.

I followed the instructions, came back with the key, opened the door, and stepped silently into the empty kitchen. I tiptoed to my sister's room and saw that it was empty as well. As I stepped back in the kitchen to make my way into the living room, I felt my aunt's arms wrapped around me in an embrace. It was as if she was telling me, "Okay, here we go. I'm here with you and we are going to be okay."

It was in the living room that I saw my wife and sister having sex, right there in front of me. There was no denying it, but still my brain couldn't quite register what was happening because it was just so . . . *big*.

Finally, I heard my own voice speak. "What's going on?" I asked, even though it was incredibly clear exactly what was going on. I stammered out the same question a couple more times before finally saying, "I'll be back. Take care of my son."

I ran upstairs, grabbed all of my stuff, and left for Las Vegas, where I spent the next few weeks, hiding out and trying to figure out what to do with the rubble that was left of my life. It felt like I was trapped in a frozen state while the world continued to spin around me. I could see people around me, but I couldn't connect with them. I had already felt demolished because of my aunt's death, and now even the things about my life that had appeared to remain intact were suddenly crashing around me. I spent a lot of time crying, talking to God and to my aunt. I had never before understood the depression I sometimes saw in others around me; it just wasn't how I rolled. And now, suddenly, I got it. I felt tiny and stuck, as I watched the bustle of Vegas, with everyone else laughing and getting on with life. *Why can't you see that everything is falling apart?* I wanted to scream at all of the happy people. It felt as if I had fallen into a deep black hole that I was never going to be able to crawl my way back out of.

Never before have I felt as alone as I did then. I couldn't tell my parents what had happened because they, too, were dealing with the loss of my aunt, and it felt like this news about my sister might tear our family apart. Not to mention the fact that I felt humiliated and embarrassed. I was very concerned with the material world—with how my life *looked.* It was important to me that it at least looked like I had my shit together, and now the whole world was going to know that my life was not what it appeared to be.

Eventually, I had to return to Long Beach, where we all continued to live in that same damn duplex. My wife and sister both swore that nothing was going on—that I had happened to walk in on a onetime situation. But that just didn't feel true to me, no matter what they said. I couldn't bear to be around my sister, so I stopped going to work, despite the fact that it was my only remaining source of income. I couldn't summon up the energy to care that this material life I'd worked so hard to build was in the process of falling apart around me. I had no idea what my next move was, and this was all made worse by the fact that, despite how angry I was, I still loved my wife and sister. The love wasn't something I could just turn off, much as I wanted to.

I mainly stayed home, preferably in bed. The only time I ventured out was to see a couple of psychiatrists. Neither one of them had anything particularly useful to say, but they *did* put me on a lot of pills, which helped me stay asleep—the only state in which I felt okay.

I had no idea how to pick up the pieces or start over again, so it felt easier to surrender and lie down. I spent a lot of that time talking to Aunt Ruthie, telling her that I no longer wanted to be in this world. I wanted to be with her, at peace. As I talked, I reached out my hand to Aunt Ruthie and felt her holding mine in return, comforting me. I saw little green lights (which, as I later came to find out, some people refer to as *orbs*), surrounding my head when I was lying in bed or in the palm of my hand when I reached it out. It was weird because, aside from the fact that I was seeing random lights floating around my room, green also happened to be Aunt Ruthie's favorite color. Every now and then, the radio turned itself on. Whenever it did, a song that comforted me just happened to be playing. At the time, I figured it was the drugs creating all of these effects and sensations, but I didn't care, because this sense of connection gave me a bit of relief and I was more than happy to take whatever I could get at that point.

Since no one knew what was happening in my life, everyone assumed that I was devastated about Aunt Ruthie's death. And, of course, I was. For my entire life, she had been my protector, and now she was gone. But, to me, it didn't feel entirely like Ruthie *was* gone.

After I had been living in this state for several weeks, Aunt Ruthie's youngest daughter came to me and suggested that I go see a tarot reader. I initially responded that the last thing I needed to do was to open up the gates of hell. Even if I wasn't practicing anymore, my Catholic and Christian backgrounds had ingrained in me to steer clear of "dark" practices.

"Maybe the reader will be able to connect you with my mom," my cousin continued.

Dark arts or not, that was all I needed to hear. I was in! At the time, I didn't realize that tarot readers aren't necessarily mediums.

On the day of my reading, I walked through a beaded curtain, stepped into a dark, dusty space, and took my seat across from Annette, a sixty-something hippie-dippy woman with red hair. Annette had a cool English accent that I had to admit was kind of magical, whether I believed in magic or not (which I did not). She spoke with her head tilted to one side and was covered in jewelry made of stones and crystals that jingled and rattled a little bit every time she moved.

I really wanted this smiling woman in front of me to connect me with Aunt Ruthie, but I also had a huge wall up. I wasn't going to let Annette crack me and all of my beliefs. I sat across from her with my arms and legs tightly crossed, determined not to give her anything. But I *did* feel a simmering excitement. I wanted to talk to my aunt, and I wanted her to tell me that I was going to be okay.

Annette began shuffling her cards. She said her name and then told me to say my own three times. She pulled a card and, before she'd even laid it down on the table, she murmured, "That's strange. There's a woman coming into the room on a white cloud."

Now I was listening.

"She has a black dog with her," the reader continued.

My Rottweiler, Zoe, had died just three weeks after Aunt Ruthie.

"The woman is eating butterscotch candy."

Okay, now it was going down! Aunt Ruthie *loved* butterscotch candy. I leaned forward in rapt attention as Annette continued to talk very specifically about everything that was going on in my life at that moment. She talked about how I had been deceived by someone close to me and that there was a triangle, which indicated infidelity with someone close. She talked about all of the material things I was losing and said I would lose more—but she also told me I would gain it all back tenfold. She told me there was someone else out there for me, a life partner. Finally, Annette said, "You are only treated the way you allow people to treat you." That statement hit me like a hot iron, and I felt a rush of anger wash over me. *How had I allowed myself to be so weak?*

It was time to get out of bed.

Within the space of that single reading, I went from being afraid of tarot to viewing it as a lifeline in turbulent times. I got into the habit of visiting Annette on a weekly basis. Not everything she said was super magical like that first reading, and I didn't always walk away with new, deep insights, but I did always find comfort during a time when I desperately needed it. Annette gave me hope that there was light at the end of the tunnel and assurance that I wasn't just floating around out there on my own. I really needed that support because no one around me knew what was happening besides my sister and my wife—and neither one of them was exactly comforting. Before all of this, I had always been the type of person who gave a lot to others, both emotionally and materially. Now that I found myself with nothing to give, a lot of the people who had been around before suddenly weren't anymore. The more the people around me disappeared, the more I connected with the unseen forces in my life—with my aunt and with God. They felt like a shield of protection around me in an otherwise big and uncertain world.

Through all of this, I continued to live in that duplex with my wife and sister. My wife continued to swear that she and my sister had only been together that one time, and I continued to intuitively know that wasn't true. Still, she continued lying. Finally, I asked Annette.

"It's been happening for months," Annette told me. "You need to sit the two of them down and make it okay for them to share with you their honest truth. Don't go into the conversation angry. If you really want to know the truth, you have to give them space to tell it to you."

So I did. I sat my wife and sister down on the couch and calmly told them that it had been months now and I just needed to know the truth. "If you guys love me like you say you do," I implored them, "you'll be honest with me about how long this has been going on for."

Just like that, *boom!* It all came out. As I suspected, their relationship had been going on for months. Knowing that for a fact freed me. I knew once and for all that there was no going back. More than that, it reconfirmed for me that something greater was out there, watching my back. It felt good to understand that I was supported, even if I didn't understand exactly what or who I was being supported by. But it didn't change the fact that life as I had known it was falling apart.

My wife and I began the process of separation. I left the medical billing company to my sister and I went into bankruptcy. I officially lost everything. My cars were repossessed and, one after another, I lost all my remaining real estate investments as the market went belly up. Thankfully, I was able to remain in the duplex with Eric since my now ex-wife continued to pay the mortgage to support me and my son.

While I was in the midst of losing everything material in my life, I was also in the process of gaining back a spiritual connection I hadn't felt since I was a little kid, in the days when I had burned candles in my room and freaked out my sister. For the first time in my adult life, I was able to connect to a spirituality that didn't involve a church. My beliefs began to evolve *within* me, rather than outside of me. I felt freed up to take with me the parts of religion that worked for me and to also be okay with accepting spiritual beliefs that weren't part of any doctrine other than what felt true to me.

It wasn't a fun time, but it certainly was an important one.

ALEX'S STORY

MY PARENTS ARE FROM COLOMBIA. I WAS BORN THERE, BUT I'VE SPENT MOST OF MY life in the United States. My parents immigrated here when I was just four years old, and we spent the next several years living all over the place, depending upon where my dad's welding work took him. Over the years, this included New York, North Carolina, South Carolina, and Montana. Finally, we landed in Southern California. For the first decade of my life, it was just me and my parents moving around. Then, when I was ten years old, my brother was born and we became a family of four.

My mom is very Catholic, and my dad isn't religious at all. To this day, my mom still tries to get my dad to go to church. He always says no because, as he puts it, he and God have their own relationship, and my dad doesn't feel like he has to go to a church for them to communicate. As a kid, I went through the normal rites of passage—baptism, first communion, and all of that. For a while, I didn't think much about it, but when I was eight or nine years old and the time came for me to start going to confession, it just didn't feel right. I felt uncomfortable going into a little room with a guy I didn't know, plus I couldn't figure out how to tell the difference between sinning and being a kid. I had a lot of questions, and it felt like there weren't a lot of answers. As I got older, those questions continued to present themselves and I continued searching for answers.

When I was eighteen, my parents and brother moved back to Colombia, but I decided to stay in Southern California. It was home to me, and I knew that staying there on my own would free me from the secret I'd been keeping for so long. It felt like an opportunity to live my life the way I wanted to for the first time. I'm gay and, despite the fact that I have known this about myself since I was six years old, it wasn't something we talked about in my family. If I'm being really honest, I knew I was trans dating back to the time I was six years old, but I didn't have a name for it, and it wasn't something I consciously realized until I was older. Even if I had consciously realized it, transgenderism *certainly* wasn't something we talked about in my family—at least back then. I remember having an argument in a store with my mom when I was a kid because she wanted to buy me a T-shirt that read "I'm a Girl."

"No," I told her, picking up the "I'm a Boy" T-shirt. "I want this one. I'm not a girl."

In the end, I got the "I'm a Boy" T-shirt. Still, it wasn't until a couple of decades later, during meditation, that I was able to consciously realize and accept what had been true all along—that I didn't feel at home in my own body.

Long before that, though, I came to terms with my sexuality. Even though it wasn't something my parents and I talked about when I was growing up, it was pretty obvious that I was gay. I never had boyfriends and I always dressed very masculine. Sometimes I brought "friends" home who were women and, coincidentally, my mom never liked them. On some level, my mom knew I was gay, but she wasn't able to accept it. I can't speak for her, but I would guess that was for a combination of reasons, including the fact that homosexuality wasn't widely accepted or talked about in Colombia at the time and, also, because my mom was old-fashioned and might have believed that my sexuality was somehow a failing on her part. In all fairness, I never broached the topic, either. I didn't want to hurt my mom or cause her any sort of emotional pain.

So, when my parents moved away just as I was going to college, it felt like an opportunity for me to openly live life the way I wanted to. Because they were so far away, my sexuality was an easy topic for us to avoid from that point forward. We never talked about my relationships; they didn't ask, and I didn't bring it up. A couple of times, I brought "friends" with me to visit Colombia, but just like when I was a teenager, my parents didn't ask and I didn't tell. Occasionally, my mom asked me when I was going to get married and have kids, but the topic was easy enough to navigate. At that point, gay marriage wasn't legal, and I also didn't want to have kids.

Looking back, it's hard to imagine living such a secret life but, back then, it didn't seem like a huge deal. I didn't want to hurt my parents and, because they were so removed from my day-to-day life, I could convince myself that I was protecting them from unnecessary pain. Before cellphones, it was expensive to call Colombia, so I didn't get to talk to my family as much as I would have liked to. When I did, I wanted to keep everything as happy and positive as possible. It felt like there was never a right time, and I had plenty of excuses at my disposal.

Once my parents departed for Colombia and I was left to my own devices, I was free, but I was also alone. I never went to church anymore. It just didn't feel right. But, as a sociology major, I took a lot of classes about different religions and cultures, and loved observing and learning about different practices. I've always been very open, and various parts of every religion and culture I studied resonated with me. At a certain point, it occurred to me that I didn't have to shove my beliefs into a box labeled Catholicism, Buddhism, Kabbalah, or anything else. I could just take what worked for me from each religion, and leave what didn't behind. It dawned on me that there really were no rules outside of being a good human. *That* felt true to me.

When I was in my late thirties, a friend invited me to a religious ceremony. This particular religion was born from African slaves who had Catholicism thrust upon them when they arrived in the Americas, and who found themselves unable to practice their native religion. The slaves devised a system in which they prayed to saints who stood in for their own gods. So, for instance, while it looked to slave owners like the slaves were praying to the Virgin Mary, they were actually using her as a placeholder for their own tribal deities.

This religion has stood the test of time and evolved over the centuries. Since it cropped up in Cuba, many of its practitioners are Latinx. It is, in many ways, a very beautiful religion, and one that includes a lot of magic. This isn't surprising, because it evolved from a culture that has a tradition of rituals for the moon, river, and ocean and utilizes various herbs and plants for healing and other spiritual purposes. At ceremonies, you might see sacred drum circles, spirits that are summoned through trance, and an otherwise normal five-year-old child suddenly going into an incredibly intricate tribal dance, while balancing nine plates on their head and simultaneously spinning more in their hands. This religious practice is powerful and magical to behold. It makes sense that a lot of seekers are drawn to it. I was definitely a seeker at the point in my life when I was introduced to the practice.

Based on its roots, it's not surprising that this religion is known as a secretive belief system. I, like many others, was curious to know what those secrets were. It's a very hierarchical religion and participants are given information gradually. There is essentially a process of initiation, culminating in a big ceremony during which everyone wears white and inductees' heads are shaved. There are many steps before this, though, and being invited to a ceremony is the very first.

It felt amazing to experience something so outside of the box. More than that, I was so alone here in the United States that I loved the idea of being around a group of people who were so bonded. Even in that first ceremony, I felt very much like I was being enveloped in a spiritual family or tribe. It also felt familiar to me because of its Latinx influence. Not only that, but the ceremony also included many of the Catholic prayers that I was brought up on, such as the Our Father, recited in Spanish.

During that first ceremony, there came a point when I was given the choice to stay or leave. I couldn't resist the lure of curiosity, so I stayed . . . but I felt torn about it. It was hard to *really* make a choice in a situation where I didn't know what was going to come next. And even though I was explicitly given the choice to stay or go, it almost felt as if I was being jumped in or something.

I learned that in order to continue to practice within this belief system, I had to be initiated and, over time, move up in rank. I was curious, but I also wasn't interested in being boxed into one practice. As I continued to go to ceremonies, I felt that boxing-in start to happen.

Still, I enjoyed being around the people at the ceremonies, despite the fact that I wasn't allowed to join in on all of the gatherings, since I had not been fully initiated. Through them, I began to find a piece of myself that I previously had no idea existed. Most important, I was introduced to magic. I learned how to set up an altar and create a sacred space in my home that I could use as my church. A place where I could go to speak to God. For the first time since my parents left, I didn't feel alone anymore. I began to connect with my ancestors, including ones I had never met but somehow felt I now knew. It was a powerful time for me, and it represented a big shift in my belief system. I was profoundly grateful for that.

As I was finding my way spiritually, other areas of my life felt unsettled, too. At the time, I was employed as a social worker at a skilled nursing facility, but I wasn't really happy there anymore. Working with the sick and elderly was emotionally draining, and also very hard on my spirit. I stayed in that position for more than five years and, in that time, many of the residents and I developed deep bonds. It was incredibly difficult to arrive at work only to find out that a resident had passed, which was obviously a frequent hazard of the job. It was also tough to see some of these residents spend day after day in a little room with few or no visitors other than me. While I enjoy being the highlight of a person's day, I didn't enjoy it under those circumstances. As the emotional and spiritual weight of the job bore down on me more and more, I simultaneously felt an entrepreneurial urge bubbling up inside of me.

In the midst of all of this, my mom was diagnosed with a brain tumor. Within just a week of finding out about the tumor, my mom was wheeled into an operating room to undergo brain surgery. I wasn't able to be there. In this moment, my interest in magic switched gears. Magic felt like the only thing I could do to help my mom since I couldn't be there for her physically.

I began performing rituals for my mother's healing that were mainly centered around candles and making offerings to the mountains and ocean. Prior to this, all of the magic I had been doing revolved around things that weren't nearly as critical as my mom's life. In some ways, I felt out of my depth, but I decided to rely on my instinct, rather than a prescribed step-by-step process. Looking back, this was a big moment for me because it's when I learned to listen to my own intuition and follow what felt right to me. I came to deeply believe that, when it comes to ritual, what matters most is the connection I make with and energy I put toward God and spirit—not the specifics of the offering. Once this dawned on me, I got really serious about faith and magic; the type of faith and magic that, while inspired by a variety of different sources, are mostly based on my own intuition. You could say I built a temple in my own home, in myself.

After a while, my mom started getting better. Was it the magic that healed her, or the medical attention? Of course I don't know, but I believe it was some combination of the two. I'd like to think that all of the energy and focused attention on her healing I put out there helped in some way. What I know for sure is that my practice made *me* feel better during a very difficult time. It made me feel supported during a time when I was deeply alone. The whole experience instilled in me the mindset that when we strongly put our faith and belief in something, it *does* impact the results.

By the end of my mom's journey, I had completely separated myself from any type of organized religion or official ceremonies. I realized that, for as much as I wanted spiritual community and, in some ways, longed for the energy of a group in celebration and prayer, I didn't *need* it to have a spiritual practice. I am very grateful for the teachers in my past who instilled in me a deeply rooted faith that spirituality should never, ever bring us into conflict with our own principles and personal beliefs. Who showed me that it's okay to find your own religion within the walls of your own being and that your spiritual journey doesn't have to include anyone other than yourself.

MAGIC AND MANIPULATION

There is a fine line when it comes to offering magic to others, and the best way to think about it is by drawing a correlation with religion. Most of us understand that it is not okay to force our religious views or practices upon others. However, many of us *will* pray for others who need some sort of healing. Even though magic is not a religion, you can think of this particular aspect in the same way. It's not ever okay to attempt to force your magic on anyone else, no matter how good your intentions. They have to opt in. However, it *is* okay to offer blessings and prayers to those who are in need when it serves their highest good. For example, if you have an ill parent or a grieving friend, offering healing blessings is appropriate. Foisting a ritual upon them that they don't want any part in is not okay.

Once people discover the power of magic in their own lives, there is often the desire to want to share it with their loved ones. Of course! You realize how awesome it is to invite this sort of power and support into your own life, and you want those closest to you to have a similar experience. We've seen many people come from this place and try to somehow "sneak" magic through to their loved ones in the form of a magic candle or crystal, passing that item off as something far different from and simpler than what it actually is.

Here's the thing: That doesn't work, regardless of how well intended the sentiment behind it is.

Magic is all about free will. It's about permission and signing on.

Hopefully it goes without saying that since magic should not be used on others without their permission for good intentions, it should certainly never be used on anyone else with mal-intent. Magic should only ever be used with the highest good in mind—that includes both your own highest good and theirs. It's also worth mentioning that just because you think it's in your ex's highest good to dump his girlfriend and return to you . . . well, it doesn't exactly work like that. That's a violation of free will—even if you happen to be right, which, of course, you are.

As my mom recovered and things settled, I started to more actively reevaluate my career. As I searched for a way out, I was introduced to a real estate lender. The market was hot and this woman told me that her company was hiring and there was a lot of money to be made. It felt like my prayers were being answered and this was the escape hatch I had been looking for. I took a leap of faith and began working for a broker. In just a short period of time, I was able to save up enough money to invest in and buy quite a few properties during that era in the 2000s when it was possible to get a loan with no money down.

Of course you know how this story ends. Just before I turned forty, the market started its descent.

TWO PATHS CONVERGE

AS WE WERE ORGANIZING OUR GARAGE RECENTLY, WE UNEARTHED A PICTURE OF the two of us together on a trip long before we actually knew each other. Neither of us remembers the picture being taken—or even being on the trip together, for that matter—but there it is: the two of us sitting around the same table, each of us with our girlfriend at the time.

Our paths first crossed long before we got together, back when Marlene was dating her first girlfriend in the wake of leaving Eric's father. As Marlene puts it, she was into doing "all of the gay things" back then. Her girlfriend ran in the same crowd as Alex, so the two of us often ended up at the same place, even though we weren't friends. Despite the fact that we never really talked, we were aware of each other. More specifically, Marlene was very aware of Alex; Alex was not very aware of Marlene.

When Marlene is in a relationship, she commits. Despite that, she remembers feeling a ping the first time she saw Alex. It felt . . . weird. From that point on, Marlene made a concerted effort to avoid so much as looking at Alex.

Marlene's not usually a drinker, but during the time when she was healing from the fallout of Aunt Ruthie's death and the breakup of her marriage, Marlene went out to a bar with a friend of hers named Lauren. Marlene had two drinks, which meant she was drunk. Later on that night, Marlene and Lauren were back at home looking through old pictures when they came across one with Alex in it.

"*Oh,* I had a crush on her!" Marlene laughed.

"On Alex?" Lauren asked.

"You *know* her?!"

"Yeah, she's my friend, and I think she's single."

In their drunken state, Marlene and Lauren started scheming. They decided it was a good idea for Lauren to set up a "casual" get-together that would serve the purpose of getting Marlene and Alex in the same room together. Marlene took the conversation very seriously. Lauren, as it turns out, did not.

A few days later, Marlene followed up. "Did you call Alex yet?" she asked Lauren.

"Oh, you really wanted me to call her?"

"*Yes!*" Marlene replied.

Lauren called Alex, but Alex didn't return the call. A few days later, Lauren called Alex again. Still no response.

While Alex and Lauren were friends, they hadn't talked in a few years, so whenever Alex saw the unknown number come up on her phone, she bumped it straight to voicemail. Alex listened to Lauren's messages, but she's not great at answering the phone, much less returning voicemails. Alex was confused about why Lauren sounded so increasingly desperate to get ahold of her, but it still took a while for Alex to return the call. Finally, she did.

When the two women spoke, Lauren told Alex that she was getting a bunch of friends from back in the day together at a bar they all used to frequent. Alex asked who was going, and Lauren listed off Marlene and a few other names Alex didn't know. Not only that, but the bar was located in Long Beach, a forty-five-minute drive from where Alex lived in

L.A. Still, it sounded important to Lauren, so Alex promised she would try to make it, but also warned Lauren that her mom was visiting from Colombia, which might make it difficult to get away.

The day of the "gathering" came. Marlene pulled out all the stops: She got a new outfit, got her hair done, and put extra effort into her makeup. She arrived at the bar jittery and full of nervous anticipation. As Marlene and Lauren sat there, it got later and later—ten o'clock, then eleven o'clock, then midnight, and still no Alex. It was right around midnight when Marlene realized that Alex wasn't coming. By then, Marlene had moved along the spectrum from excited to annoyed to deflated to angry. Finally, at one a.m., Marlene asked Lauren for Alex's number. When Alex answered the phone, Marlene laid into her from right there in the middle of the bar, with the music bumping in the background. Alex was confused about who exactly this woman telling her off was, and had no idea what she was talking about. Still, though, Alex was nice.

"I'm really sorry," Alex explained. "I didn't realize that I was supposed to meet someone. I never would have blown you off. Why don't you have fun and give me a call when you get home? We can talk. You have my number, just give me a call."

All great love stories begin just like this, right?

That night, we ended up talking until five o'clock in the morning. We did the same thing the next night and the night after that. Over the next few months, these conversations became a part of our nightly routine. We shared everything and grew close quickly. Both of us were going through it, thanks to the crashing economy and our own personal struggles. We started to rely on that supportive voice on the other end of the line at the end of long, hard days. But since Marlene was in Long Beach and Alex was in Los Angeles, our relationship was limited to the phone. It was almost like a more analog version of online dating, except Marlene knew who Alex was and what she looked like, but Alex didn't have any idea who was on the other end of the line. Also, Alex didn't really think of it as dating. She was still living the single life, out at the clubs and bars most nights. The only difference was that now she came home from the bar or club and talked on the phone with Marlene.

There was also the fact that both of us were holding on to a lot of fresh baggage. Aunt Ruthie's death and the breakup of Marlene's marriage were less than six months in the past. Alex had recently been through the roller-coaster ride of her mom's brain tumor, and was feeling depressed and afraid because of the impact the economy was having on her livelihood. Both of us were losing properties as the real estate market continued to dwindle. Because we were just friends, we were able to be very open with each other about what was going on in our lives. We didn't hold back in the way we might have if we were trying to impress a potential romantic partner. But even if it was just a friendship at that point, it was still an important relationship for both of us. Most nights, our conversations lasted until the sun came up the following morning. Our phone calls were a safe space for each of us and we created a support system for each other during a time when we both really needed it.

A couple of months after we'd begun talking, Marlene invited Alex to a Fergie concert in Vegas. We drove the four and a half hours from Los Angeles to Vegas and spent a couple of days together in person for the first time. It was very comfortable because we'd already spent so much time talking. We knew each other inside and out before we even really met. It all felt very platonic, though.

The day of the concert, we got dressed up and went down to the hotel lobby, ready to go. It wasn't until that point that Marlene looked at the concert tickets and realized she had the wrong date. The concert was actually the following night, and Alex had to be back in Los Angeles before then. Instead of going to the show, we ended up on a rooftop bar. All this time, it had seemed to Marlene that Alex had no interest in moving into anything more serious than the bar scene and active dating life. But now here we were having deeper conversations and feelings. Suddenly, it seemed, Alex was at a point in her life when she wanted to settle down into a meaningful relationship.

The concert was a wash but we haven't left each other's side since that day.

Becoming a couple felt *right.* Both of us appreciated the fact that we had each other, especially since we were each coming out of a period during which we felt isolated in our own ways. But the fact that we were together didn't mean that all our problems suddenly disappeared. In fact, it felt more like our problems doubled in size because Alex's problems became Marlene's problems and vice versa. Neither of us had any income, and things were hard. Marlene was still wading through depression, and had let everything go into bankruptcy as a result, despite the fact that she had always been so responsible, the person who never broke. Meanwhile, Alex was losing one investment property after another as the market rolled downward.

Alex moved into Marlene's house shortly after that trip to Vegas when we mutually decided that renting out Alex's home and living together would help ease our collective financial burden. When Alex arrived, Marlene started the process of weaning off the medication she'd been taking since life seemingly fell apart several months before. This meant that she had to deal with feeling everything again, including anger. With the numbness suddenly gone, Marlene found herself searching for something. Although she had long since left both Catholicism and Christianity behind, she still carried some of the beliefs and practices with her. This included a fear of magic and the dark forces it might usher in. While the tarot reader had been a source of relief, Marlene was still wary of anything that tapped into energies she didn't understand or had been taught to steer clear of.

At first, Marlene kept a safe distance from the altar Alex set up in their home and the candles she purposefully burned. Alex did all of this quietly, but Marlene suspected there was something more behind whatever it was Alex was practicing. Still, Marlene was increasingly intrigued, especially because she saw that whatever it was Alex was doing seemed to bring her peace. Alex would sometimes join Marlene when she prayed Catholic prayers for comfort; every now and then, Alex would quietly burn a candle as the two of us prayed. Marlene didn't know exactly what Alex was doing, and she didn't want to ask, so she just continued to pray over the candles.

A few months passed, and Marlene started to notice that things were shifting a little bit for Alex. Things were happening—strange things. Like, Alex would receive random, unexplained checks, even including a check from the IRS at one point. Who gets random checks from the IRS? Or rebate checks that Alex had filed for months ago came in at the precise moment she needed the exact amount they were cut for. It was clear that, inexplicably, roads were opening for her. Marlene suspected there was some link between whatever was happening over the altar and candles and the forward motion and saving graces in Alex's life. It finally reached a point where Marlene couldn't stand not knowing exactly what Alex was doing, so she asked despite her fear. When Alex explained that she was setting intentions over candles and presenting offerings to spirit through her altar as well as using it as a sacred space to pray, something clicked for Marlene. It suddenly didn't seem so scary anymore. So we began to pray with intention over the candles together. We prayed for help and guidance out of our situation, we prayed not to be stuck. We prayed for answers and a new path to follow.

Before you know it, Marlene had returned to the fanaticism she had experienced during her days in the Christian church. But this time, she had a partner. Every single day, we prayed together at our altars and over our candles. Marlene prayed for the anger to lift and the next phase of life to present itself. Alex prayed for a way of getting by that didn't include going back to social work, and of getting out of the vulnerable state she found herself in, being so far away from her family and without anyone to fall back on. Through this, our bond grew even tighter. We built an energetic tie between the two of us, although we probably couldn't have explained it that way at the time.

As the months went by, we continued praying over the candles and started incorporating little rituals of our own as they occurred to us. As Marlene's interest grew, Alex introduced her to more and more magical principles. For instance, Alex explained the meaning and energy behind the colored bracelets that she wore and frequently swapped out, as well as the numbers and herbs that she incorporated into various rituals. Alex shared her belief in spirit guides, what they did, and how they could be incorporated into ritual. Every day, Marlene grew more and more open to ideas she had never considered before and took her own practice of prayer and ritual more seriously.

After an entire lifetime of shutting it out, Marlene was able to share with Alex her belief that she had been in contact with people who had passed, both as a child and more recently with Aunt Ruthie. Alex accepted this without question and, for Marlene, that felt like being given permission to open up to and embrace her mediumship abilities. Marlene was able to release that feeling of being in conflict with herself, which had always plagued her in the days when she had ascribed to Catholicism and Christianity. Since leaving the Christian church nearly a decade ago, there had been a void in Marlene's life. It felt like that was filled by opening up to spirituality again, which had always been an important (and often problematic) missing piece in the puzzle of her life. Alex had shown Marlene that spirituality extended far beyond religion and didn't require subscribing to a specific faith or set of practices. It felt incredibly freeing.

At the time, neither of us really had a name for what we were doing with our altars, candles, and prayers. We just knew these practices made us feel better. They gave us hope for the future and made us feel more connected, both to one another and to something bigger than us. That felt really good, but it still didn't change the fact that we were going to go broke and lose all of our remaining investments if we didn't figure out a way through this.

CHAPTER TWO

OUR INTUITION LED US THERE

WE NEVER HAD TO GO ON PUBLIC ASSISTANCE DURING THE GREAT RECESSION, BUT there were plenty of times when we were close. We still had a little bit of income coming in from our constantly diminishing rentals, along with some savings. Those savings included money for Eric's college tuition, so we didn't want to actually dig into it, but knowing the money was there provided a small sense of security.

We spent a lot of time praying for guidance, but we were also willing to do whatever it took to get by—which, for us, included yard sales (we're talking *huge* organized yard sales that, over time, evolved into a makeshift store in our garage) and starting a trucking company, where we served as the middleman, setting up businesses with contracted drivers. Random? Yes. But even though these things didn't light us on fire and weren't how we wanted to live our lives in the long run, they fed us and paid our bills. Even so, it was a pretty hand-to-mouth existence for quite some time, and not sustainable.

We continued to pray and chant for at least thirty minutes every day, and sometimes for up to two hours. We would open up different prayer books from a wide range of religions and read whatever we happened to flip to. Whatever that passage was, we took it as our message for the day and moved in that direction. We started playing a game, not really understanding that what we were actually doing was strengthening our intuition. It was silly, really, but we loved it. For example, Alex would say, "What chocolate bar am I thinking of?" And then we would both freak out when Marlene correctly guessed, "Almond Joy!"

Meanwhile, we visited Marlene's tarot reader whenever we could afford to, but it was expensive at $60 a pop. We could stretch $60 out for five days! After a while, it occurred to us that maybe we should learn to read our own cards. So we got a deck of tarot cards, despite the fact that we had no clue how to interpret them. Little by little, we learned how to read tarot cards—but not in the traditional way of flipping through books to study the meanings of various symbols. Instead, we homed in on our own inner voices to figure out what the cards meant to us. We practiced this over and over and over again until we built up confidence in our ability to interpret the messages and visions we were receiving in our mind's eye. When we wanted answers, we talked to our guides and angels and asked them what they wanted to tell us through the cards. One day, they told us that the repo man was coming. We decided to park our car a mile away from the house to avoid having it seized. Unfortunately, the angels weren't as specific as they could have been. They were right that it was repo day, but they could have offered a bit more guidance about what we should do to *avoid* him, because the car was gone that evening anyway.

At the time, we had no idea at all that we were basically in training for a new life that had not yet revealed itself. Let's be serious: We didn't even know what the word *metaphysical* meant back then. We were just curious, and all of this stuff we were dabbling in seemed fun and interesting. It also served as a momentary distraction from our very real problems and gave us a small sense of control over a series of circumstances that felt completely *out* of our control.

When we found ourselves in situations in which we needed guidance we could trust, we would scrape our coins together to visit the tarot reader, regardless of the cost. That shows how much trust we had in tarot, because every single dollar we had meant a lot at that moment in time.

During one reading we booked in a moment of desperation, the tarot reader caught us off guard. "I see a business here," she said. "This is something you guys have been talking about."

We looked at each other, having a silent conversation over the table.

At that point in time, our version of date night was cooking dinner at home, then walking around the corner to the 7-Eleven to buy lottery tickets. We were really into it. Alex regularly researched statistics on lottery tickets—which tickets were new, which ones still had a high number of winning tickets out there and up for grabs. We even had a special keychain with a scratching tool at the end of it. We absolutely wanted to win money when we played the lottery—and sometimes we did, $100 here, $500 there—but we also loved dreaming about what we would do if we *did* win a million dollars. The dream we collectively landed on and talked about the most was opening up a spiritual detox center. At this center, no religion would be turned away, and no one's vulnerability would be taken advantage of. We would hire authentic tarot card readers so that people could experience the power of communicating with something bigger without the fear that the wool was being pulled over their eyes for the sake of making a quick buck. The details of this spiritual detox center were very clear to us—we knew what it would feel and look like. We could see it all very clearly. But just because we could see it didn't mean that we were willing to take the leap and make this center a reality. It was just a dream and, really, how *could* we?

In those long seconds of silence around that tarot table, the two of us were making a decision. Were we willing to make this spiritual detox center more than a dream? Because both of us knew that if we brought something to the table for our spirit guides to consult on, that meant we had to be serious about it. We had to be willing to take action on the next flip of the cards if that's what spirit required.

Finally, Marlene said to Alex, "Should I ask?"

It was like there was some sort of telecommunication happening, because Alex knew exactly what question Marlene was referring to. "Yes, ask," she replied.

The reader flipped the cards once again and looked down on them. To this day, both of us still remember the look on the reader's face—it was as if she'd *seen* something. The tone of her voice became stern and matter-of-fact as she said at last, "This is your destiny. During this time, you will have to ask for help. You two are always the givers, but now it's time to receive. The angels will appear to help you, but you need to be open to receiving."

In that moment, Marlene felt chills go down her back and neck and Alex felt as if a bucket of cold water had been dumped over her. We didn't have a business plan and, even more than that, we weren't readers or healers ourselves. We were just two people who'd had a good experience with metaphysical practices. Although, back then, we wouldn't have even thought of these as metaphysical experiences because we didn't know the word! *That's* how unprepared we were.

As it turned out, the reader had more to say. "One last thing: You will lose everything before spirit shows up and you gain it back. Don't let fear creep in. Know that, while you'll lose everything, you will receive it all back tenfold."

The two of us were completely tripped out on the car ride home. How could we possibly make this work? We had already sold off pretty much everything of value we owned. All we had left to work with was

Marlene's son's money and Alex's house in Silver Lake, which she was renting out. Alex felt numb at the weight of it all, and Marlene cried.

"You can cry today," Alex told Marlene, "but you're not going to cry tomorrow."

"But what are we going to do?" Marlene wailed.

"I don't know, but we're going to figure it out," Alex replied. After a few moments of silence driving down the Pacific Coast Highway, she spoke again. "Okay, I'm going to let the Silver Lake house go. We'll short-sell it." Already Alex was releasing control, despite the fact that she is the least impulsive person ever. Alex won't even buy a pair of tennis shoes until she has checked twenty different websites, visited ten different stores, tried a bunch of shoes on, brought a pair home, tried them on, returned them, and thought and researched some more. Now here she was, ready to release her final asset based on the tarot reader's guidance.

Seeing this out-of-character behavior from Alex provided Marlene with the strength she needed to take a leap. If Alex was in, Marlene was going to be in, too.

Before the day was done, Alex was already looking for a retail space to rent. Nothing screams fun like trying to rent a storefront in a bad market with a bankruptcy on your credit report. That didn't stop us, though. In our date-night dreaming sessions, we had envisioned that the place meant for us would be somewhere by the water, so we started our search in places like Redondo and Manhattan Beach, but nothing we saw felt right. A few days went by and, as we continued looking, we performed even more rituals than usual. We picked specific flowers to offer up on our altar, did road-opening spells (see the Road-Opening Bath on page 217), and called upon God, angels, and our ancestors. We asked them to take away our fear, to clear the way for us, and to take our blinders off so that we could see the way forward more clearly.

As the meticulous one, Alex was in charge of finding us a place. But five days into our search, Marlene happened to stumble upon a Craigslist listing for a little house up on a hill in the Echo Park area of Los Angeles. The listing featured a picture of a weed-infested foreground and a guy pushing a shopping cart in the background. Unimpressive as it was, Marlene had a feeling about the property, and Alex added it to her extensively researched list at Marlene's insistence. That was the extent of Marlene's property search.

"Don't you want to look some more?" Alex asked, when Marlene immediately got off Craigslist and returned to Facebook to keep playing FarmVille (remember, it was 2009!).

"Nope," Marlene shook her head, now fully engrossed in feeding her virtual horses. "That's the one."

The very next day, we went to look at the little house in Echo Park. We greeted the realtor in the parking lot by telling her we wanted to rent this home for our business. Before she could even get a word in edgewise, we vomited everything out, telling her all about how we wanted to open up a spiritual detox center and to help as many people as we could in the process.

"Whoa!" the realtor said when we finally let her get a word in. "I'm not actually the decisionmaker here. I don't own this place. I'm just here to show it to you. And . . . don't you want to take a look inside before you make a decision?"

We went inside, even though it felt like a waste of time to us. The linoleum floors were covered with industrial carpeting. The wood-paneled walls were dark, the shelving was dark, the energy was dark. Everything was dark and dusty. The realtor explained that the property had served as an attorney's office for forty-five years. In the nine months since the attorney, Phillip, had passed away, this place had been sitting vacant.

Despite our enthusiasm about the space and the fact that it had been empty for so long, the realtor seemed dubious about our prospects. The house was owned by Phillip's eighty-year-old wife, Evelyn, who had apparently already turned down many rental applicants before us. For as dark and dusty as the house was, Phillip had loved the place and Evelyn felt very protective of the property. The realtor explained that Evelyn really wanted another attorney to take it over, but one hadn't yet turned up. "I'll see what I can do," she half-heartedly promised us.

The next day, the realtor emailed to let us know Evelyn wanted to meet with us. Holy shit! We needed to do some major magic. Our preparation for the meeting consisted of the two of us lighting every single candle we could find in the house. We poured a ton of honey over the candles to sweeten Evelyn up. We placed pennies on top of the honey for abundance. We set up a little toy house to represent the rental on our altar and prayed to the spirits, letting them know that this was the house we wanted for our business. We told them that if they wanted this to happen—if this spiritual detox center was our destiny—then we needed a miracle to put blinders up around our bad credit and meager bank account. We understood that, beyond this, the situation was out of our hands. We could work on behalf of spirit, but we couldn't manipulate the reality of how the world works.

Evelyn arrived at our meeting all dolled up and dressed to the nines. She was a tiny, beautiful woman with a very powerful energy, and so chic with her purse and little heels. From the second we saw her, we realized that this was not a woman we could bullshit (which, quite frankly, was our plan, simply because it was the only one we could think of). It was immediately clear that the only way to win Evelyn over would be to look her straight in the eyes and pour our hearts out.

As we walked through the house with Evelyn, it was impossible to tell whether she liked us or not. That woman has an incredible poker face. We chatted about our vision throughout the entire tour. When we got into the kitchen, we told Evelyn about our plans to make tea to serve to customers as they waited for their tarot readings because tea is so soothing and harmonizing. Evelyn responded by telling us about a tea recipe that had been passed down through her family. "I'll give it to you," she said.

That's when we knew we were in.

Sure enough, at the end of our meeting Evelyn looked us both straight in the eye and said, "I'm going to give you a chance." What we didn't know at the time was that, in addition to being a lawyer, Phillip had also been a hypnotist. Our spiritual detox center was built on a vibration he had already established on the property. We also didn't know then that Philip and Evelyn's son had died on precisely the same day as Aunt Ruthie had.

"That's all we need," we promised Evelyn, nearly tripping over ourselves with joy and excitement. Very short-lived joy and excitement because a few minutes after we parted ways with Evelyn, the realtor called to tell us that she was sending an application for us to fill out and that they would then run our credit.

You probably won't be surprised that our response was to go home and do more magic. A *lot* more magic. We put the application on the altar and prayed with all our might before sending it in.

Of course we'll never know exactly why, but, spoiler alert: We got the place, and our credit was never brought up—despite the fact that we had a bankruptcy on our report.

And, thus, the House of Intuition was born. When Alex first blurted out the name, Marlene felt those familiar chills run up and down her back. This idea of intuition was at the heart of everything we wanted to offer people. For a while, we considered calling our new business The Psychic House, but it just didn't feel right. The word *psychic* can conjure up fears and stereotypes, and that was the exact opposite of what we wanted to do. We had benefited so much from the intuition of tarot readers in our own lives, and we wanted others to have access to that same sort of powerful insight in a nonintimidating setting. We wanted people who had the same fears Marlene initially had to have a place they felt safe and comfortable walking into. We wanted others to experience intuition as a gateway to greater spiritual experiences and a sense of connection, much as we had.

Now that we had found a space to open our little shop, we were confronted with a new set of challenges, including the small matter of having to put down thousands of dollars all at once for the security deposit, in addition to the first month of rent. Obviously, we didn't exactly have that money lying around. Marlene cried as we sat Eric down and asked if it was okay to crack into his college fund, something we had tried so hard to avoid. Finally, we had reached the point where there were no other options; there was nothing left to sell. We promised that we would do our very best to pay it back, but also warned him that there was a chance we could lose it all.

"I'll figure it out," he assured us.

With that out of the way, there were still other things to figure out, like how to deal with the fact that the Echo Park property was a mess. Luckily, we had people. Those angels the tarot reader had told us about came through, and we had no other choice but to receive their gifts. Marlene was still in contact with a contractor from her days of flipping real estate. Before everything crashed, she had given him a lot of work, and, along the way, he had become like family. He offered to help us get the place together for no charge outside of supplies, as did another friend who loved gardening. Alex had an electrician friend who also helped us out from the goodness of his heart. Meanwhile, the two of us got down to business, pulling up the flooring and painting everything in sight to brighten the place up.

If you know the clean black-and-white aesthetic of House of Intuition today, it would probably be jarring to see how different this first store looked. Basically, there was no aesthetic at all, we just did what we could. This included lots of mustard walls and cheap, shabby, repurposed furniture thrown together in one big mishmash. Our go-to solution to jazz everything up was gold spray paint. That would do the trick, we figured!

One by one, our problems were being solved. But the fact remained that we were opening up a business built around tarot readers, despite the fact that we weren't readers ourselves, nor did we know any. So we went where anyone would go to find credible tarot readers: Craigslist! We knew exactly what we were looking for, though, and that was not showy, mystical, crystal-ball-toting characters, but normal people who were tapped into their gift of intuition. We wanted them to be humble, real, and no-bullshit.

We got plenty of responses to our Craigslist ad (after all, we *were* posting in L.A.), but we hadn't stopped to account for how we would interview for this type of position. Ultimately, we realized that the only way to find our people was to have applicants give us readings.

On the first day of interviews, we lined up several readings in a row, not considering the fact that these weren't exactly normal get-to-know-you meetings we could knock out in thirty minutes. We held the interviews at the shop, which didn't have electricity yet, so as the day went on and the sun began to sink, we lit the space with candles. It was all very mystical—unintentionally so, but mystical nonetheless. In addition to tarot readers, other types of healers showed up to offer their services as well. One woman went up to Alex and very dramatically pulled energy out of her solar plexus, then tossed it into a bucket. We couldn't figure out what the hell was going on, and began to wonder what we had gotten ourselves into. By the end of the day, our energy was completely drained and we even felt a little bit nauseous. For the first time, both of us truly understood how real energy is. It was also one of the first times we had to use our own intuition in a very practical way. Résumés aren't very useful when it comes to tarot readers. The only thing we could base our hires on—outside of our experience in the readings—was our gut feeling about whether or not a person was the right match for us, how authentic they were, and if they were coming from a heart space rather than a place of ego.

Looking back, it's so interesting to see how we were propelled through the process of building something we didn't fully understand and certainly weren't qualified to do. It was as if Alex was in a trance the entire time, doing instead of researching like she always does. It was like we were pawns for spirit, channeling what they were giving us and going where they were guiding us. It makes sense that for HOI to be the type of all-embracing place it has grown into, it *had* to be opened by people like us—people who were unattached and didn't consider themselves to be experts or gurus. People who weren't married to any sort of beliefs or practices. We had no ego attached to the store. We still don't.

Day after day, we worked our asses off to get the shop ready to open. It got to the point where we were both in physical pain. As it got closer to opening day, Alex started to talk about how she felt weird.

Marlene, who was exhausted, too, encouraged Alex to power through until the opening, when we could finally get some rest. Then, one morning, Alex walked into the bedroom to tell Marlene that there was blood in her urine. We had no insurance, yet there we found ourselves at County Hospital. By the time we arrived, Alex was in a ton of pain, which was doubly scary because one of Alex's defining features is that she has a very high pain threshold. It turns out that Alex had a bad infection that got into her kidneys and contaminated her blood. Alex was admitted to the hospital, where she stayed for the next eight days, heavily sedated on morphine. She had pushed herself too far, and it was scary. Nonetheless, as soon as she was out of the hospital, Alex was up and running at full speed once again.

Remember how the tarot reader told us that we would lose everything before spirit showed up? Well, it turns out she was right.

We did successfully open HOI with our little troop of tarot readers ready to roll and offer spiritual refuge to those who needed it. At that point, we felt very strongly about not selling products. Even if we hadn't felt like that, we wouldn't have known what to sell anyway. All of our own personal spiritual practices revolved around candles and the other little rituals that we made up as we went. But it never occurred to us that people would be even remotely interested in that kind of thing. Even if it had occurred to us, we didn't think of ourselves as people who were qualified to provide others with any sort of guidance. We were the people who *needed* guidance!

On top of what we perceived as our own spiritual ignorance was the fact that we had just been burned by the materialistic world and had no intention of contributing to or entangling ourselves in it. We had always envisioned HOI as a spiritual retreat, *not* as a store in which to sell products. The last thing we wanted to do was to receive money in exchange for anything related to spirituality. Instead, we wanted to support people in their faith and to help them lead better, happier lives. As an afterthought, we had a small selection of products for sale, things we thought were cool like incense and candles. Not the kind of magic candles we practiced with at home; just candles that smelled good. Oh, and we also had a random purse for sale that was left over from our yard sale days. Shockingly, that never sold, but it says a lot about our "retail strategy" at the time.

The purse wasn't the only thing that didn't sell; nothing did for the first eight months we were in business. A few customers came in for readings, but not enough to pay the rent. Every now and then, someone would wander into our shop and ask for random things, usually rocks and crystals. We had no idea what they were talking about. Other times, people asked for incense—but not the kind we had. They wanted temple incense and resin. Again, we had no clue.

Our lack of fiscal viability wasn't helped by the fact that it didn't occur to us until several weeks after opening to put a sign out on the sidewalk to make it clear that up the twenty-one-step stairway was a business, not a house. When that finally dawned on us, we made a sign that read: Your Intuition Led You Here. Before that, we just had a painting of a lotus in the garden area in front of the house. Even with the new sign, though, people still walked in and asked, "What is this place?"

Marlene spent a lot of time crying, believing that she had lost all of her son's money. Alex went numb. We had to take Eric out of private school and put him into public school so that we could make the mortgage on Marlene's duplex. Eventually we weren't able to pay that, so we started receiving eviction notices and went into foreclosure. For a few months there, we had to go on food stamps. All of our chips were in at HOI, and we found ourselves in a very, very precarious situation.

We did the only thing we knew to do, which was to stay in a deep state of prayer. We sat in the store and visualized a line of people walking up and into it. We nailed down railroad stakes at each corner of the store to secure its energetic vibration, prayed at each corner, then threw money on the ground around the house to usher in abundance (you can find this ritual, Anchor Your Home, on page 145). On our altar, we offered our ancestors and spirit guides coffee and sponge cake to connect with them and express our gratitude (see the Blessing and Gratitude Ritual for Ancestors on page 181), to foster a give and take. We gave what we could from the material world in hopes that spirit and our ancestors would offer us what they could from the spirit world. We told them that we had faith in them, no matter what happened. And we did. But it was still scary.

While HOI didn't generate a profit—or even sustenance, for that matter—we did begin to foster connections. As the months passed, a little community of regulars gravitated around HOI. Of course they didn't come in to buy things because there wasn't much of anything to buy, but they did come in on a normal basis just to say hello. It never occurred to us to treat these new friends as a client base, because our connection felt so profound—like we were a spiritual family. Even if we had decided to treat them as clients, it didn't change the fact that we had nothing to sell them that they were interested in. In retrospect, it's fitting that our first storefront was in a house rather than a more traditional retail space, because we wanted it to be a home for spiritual seekers and practitioners.

We welcomed every single person who came through our door and, before long, people from the neighborhood got into the habit of popping in to sit down and chat with us. All of us spent a lot of time in the waiting room, a space that included a big sofa and chairs for the specific intent of gathering and lounging. Everyone who came was greeted with tea and the inviting smell of burning incense. In turn, our guests brought flowers, pictures of their deceased loved ones, money to place on the mantel of our fireplace, and other offerings to lay at our altar, where we allowed them to burn candles. Together, we all prayed to our spirits and guides.

On Sundays, HOI stayed open even though every other business on the street was closed. It naturally evolved into a church of sorts for this group of regulars that craved a safe, welcoming, sacred place but didn't feel connected to more traditional religion. We shared our struggles with the people in our burgeoning community, and they told us about theirs. For us, it felt natural and therapeutic. To our visitors, HOI felt like a warm, hospitable space, without any ulterior motives. For all of us, it generated a sense that we were in it together, and the connection quickly grew genuine and deep. For example, one time a woman from the neighborhood walked through the door sobbing to the point where she was heaving and we couldn't understand what she was trying to say. Finally, we were able to understand that her step-daughter had died the previous night, and she had come to us because she didn't know where else to go.

In many ways, HOI was becoming the spiritual detox center that the two of us had dreamed of. The problem is that it wasn't sustainable.

From this circle of regulars, we also brought in more healers in addition to the tarot readers. Gone were the days of Craigslist—thank God! Now our healers found us. For example, there was a guy in the neighborhood named Dom who started spending a lot of time at HOI. He often talked about how he was learning sound therapy with crystal bowls. Marlene was increasingly receiving messages, and she got one about him. "Dom, you are going to use sound to be a healer," she told him one day.

"No, I'm not!" he replied, laughing.

Turns out Dom was wrong. In fact, Dom works at HOI to this day, doing sound bowl meditations as well as individual sound healings. We've had a lot of experiences like this, where people who are initially drawn to us as either clients or employees ultimately become healers. Almost none of them saw it coming.

We spent a lot of time sitting in circles and meditating with our healers, although the two of us didn't understand what we were doing at the time. To us, meditation was something "other" people did—people with shaved heads who sat on top of mountains. It didn't happen in a little shop in Echo Park. Without understanding what we were doing, we learned how to place our feet flat on the ground with our hands turned upward toward the sky to receive. We learned to open up our crown chakra at the top of our head as we visualized white light coming in, then pushed that light out through our hearts and into the city below us. As a group, we called out to all the people who needed us, to all of the people who were in pain, and imagined them walking into HOI. The two of us continued these practices on our own whenever we could, even if that happened during the forty-five minutes we spent driving to work from Long Beach to Echo Park. That happened a lot, since we worked at the shop from ten in the morning until ten at night every day.

Although it was a stressful time in many ways, there were plenty of moments that were fun and magical. Those moments allowed us to stay in a space of healing and to receive glimpses of hope. Being surrounded by people who were so vulnerable and open with their own struggles also reminded us that, for as tough as life had been in the recent past, we had a lot of blessings and many things to be grateful for.

The queries about the crystals continued to come from the few would-be customers who found their way into our store, so one day Marlene decided to take the matter to our altar. "All right," she said, "I'm tired of hearing about these rocks and crystals. If you guys want us to have them here, you better bring them forth and put them in my hands, because I'm not about to go shopping in a rock catalog." We weren't at all sold on the idea of dealing in crystals because we knew nothing about them. But we did know that if spirit was going to walk us down that path, we would have to hold and feel the rocks so that we could understand for ourselves what they did.

A few weeks later, the two of us went on one of our many trips to support the opening of another spiritual store, this time in Culver City. We figured that if we supported other stores, spirit would support ours, too. As was often the case, we spent most of our time at the opening standing in a corner feeling awkward. We didn't speak the same language as these people; we didn't know about Reiki or chanting or fairies or crystals. Theirs was an entirely different type of spirituality from our own.

However, we *were* intrigued by the fact that this particular store had rocks and crystals all over the place. Coincidence?

After a while, a woman approached us and introduced herself as Shelly. She asked what we did and we told her about our little store.

Shelly perked up. "Oh, do you guys sell crystals?"

Argh! There was that damn question again. Marlene was so sick of the topic that she couldn't hide her sarcasm. "No. Why? Do you want to sell us some? Out of a catalog or something?"

CREATING A SACRED CIRCLE

While spirituality is intensely personal, that doesn't mean it has to be practiced alone. One of our favorite things to do is to create sacred circles, much like we did in the early days of HOI—and even before that, when we were just a circle of two, playing psychic games or praying together.

Begin by clearing the space where you are sitting with sage, palo santo, incense, or resin. By doing this, you clear space for the energies that you want to invite in and keep those that you don't want out of the circle.

Open with a prayer (it doesn't have to be religious) or affirmation to bring everyone in the circle into a sacred mindset. Close your eyes, and sit with your feet planted on the floor to ground you, hands open and facing up to receive. Designate one person to lead the circle. That person will invite in spirit and white light as the rest of the group visualizes it happening.

Create a safe, open space where anyone sitting in the circle who has a message or sees a vision can share it with the group. For example, someone might say, "I see a woman with red hair and a bit of a gap between her front teeth who is a little bit overweight standing in a field." This practice simultaneously allows everyone involved to practice connecting and to receive affirmation in a safe space, while also allowing other participants to receive messages and other communication.

We always find it helpful to take notes during circles because you never know who these messages are meant for or will resonate with. Perhaps the message isn't meant for a person who is actually sitting in the circle but, instead, for one of their loved ones.

Sacred circles are powerful because they allow participants to experientially understand that there is something else out there and, most of all, that it doesn't take a guru or person with extraordinary powers to tap into that source. Each and every one of us has the ability to communicate with spirit if we make it a practice and build the muscle. Sacred circles strengthen our faith in something that we cannot see, touch, or feel. They provide a stronger sense of spirit. And, also, they're fun!

"Oh, no," Shelly replied brightly. "I come to you and bring the rocks with me so that you can feel and hold them."

That stopped Marlene in her tracks. This woman had walked up to us and basically offered exactly what we told spirit we would need if we were to walk this path.

Sure enough, a few days later, Shelly showed up at HOI and hiked up the twenty-one steps to the shop with her collection of rocks in tow. As Marlene looked through and held them, Alex stood back in the doorway. Marlene could tell just by looking at Alex that she was about to throw up.

"I don't feel right," Alex finally said. "There are too many rocks in here." At that time, neither of us understood the power crystals hold or how they might have a physical impact, but Alex intuitively knew enough to understand that they were at the root of her nausea. In fact, the energy the rocks carried in them was so powerful that Alex continued to feel off for the next three *months* after Shelly's visit—there was just so much lingering energy in our small space.

We didn't understand exactly what was happening, but it was clear that something was going on. It was also clear that the spirits had done exactly what we'd told them we needed them to do in order for us to get in the crystal game. Shelly walked Marlene through each of the crystals and explained what they were and what they did. She was a great teacher. We started to understand that crystals were yet another tool at our disposal for all the things we had come to believe in—for setting intention, enhancing intuition, and creating abundance.

We had only a tiny bit of savings left by the time Shelly came to visit with all of her shiny rocks, but Marlene decided to invest $1,500 of that money into the crystals. It bought us a single box of them. Alex (who had been too nauseous to stick around for the entire conversation about crystals) was horrified when she learned what Marlene had done. Now we had these rocks that made Alex nauseous, no idea what to do with them, and, worst of all, we weren't on the same page. In the end, that box of crystals we had spent so much money on was shoved into a closet.

A month later, when we'd spent the last of our money on rent and had no idea what to do next, we dug the box out of the closet to put the crystals out on display in the store. We had a little pond on the property, so we took some pebbles out of it and scattered them around the crystals to create a makeshift display. Then we just let the crystals be.

That's when the magic happened.

People started coming into the shop, picking up the crystals one by one, and bringing them to the register. Not a single customer even asked us what the crystals were for. Every single one of those crystals sold and, since then, HOI has never been in the red again. Those rocks turned our life around. Remember, this was in 2010. Crystals might be a draw today, but they weren't a decade ago.

It took Alex about three months to get over her crystal-induced nausea. The first day was the worst, which is probably because Shelly had a whole box of them in the store, and we only bought a fraction of them. In the weeks that followed, if Alex started feeling a bit green, she knew to put some distance between her and the crystals. And then, after several more weeks, the crystals stopped having a negative physical impact on her altogether. Today, we're always around crystals, and they don't bother Alex at all. In fact, she often carries them around with her.

In retrospect, it feels like a gift that Alex initially responded to the crystals the way she did, because we've seen the same thing happen to others since. Alex's experience has helped us identify and understand that reaction. Crystals pack powerful energy, and they impact different people in different ways. For some people that impact is subtle. For others, the impact is wholly energetic. And then, of course, for a handful of people, it's a very physical response—sometimes pleasant and, other times, not so much.

In the years since Shelly first introduced us to crystals, we've come to understand the energetic way in which they work. Today, we believe that the energies from that initial box of crystals pooled together and created an energetic force around HOI, amplifying and charging the house. It's almost as if the store became a beacon of light. Those rocks did what we couldn't have done ourselves; they were the equivalent of plugging HOI into a light socket so that people could see us. Like moths, people were drawn to that light.

FROM THAT POINT on, things grew pretty quickly. Over time, HOI shifted away from healers and moved toward emboldening people to exercise their own power and intuition. We instilled in our customers the message that they could heal themselves and create a better, more aligned life through magical tools and rituals. Go figure! We had assumed that no one else would be interested in our own magical habits when, all along, that was exactly what we needed to build our store around.

One store turned into two, which turned into ten. In less than a decade, we expanded from a single quirky little house in Echo Park to a chain of stores, first in L.A., then throughout Southern California, and now in Miami, too, with pop-up stores and an international online presence to boot. Time after time, our growth has included unlikely circumstances that can't really be explained by anything other than spirit and magic. One of us has a flash of inspiration only to be presented with signs that point us in the right direction, then the material things we need to tether that inspiration down to earth suddenly appear. The financial resources, the perfect space, and the people we need to bring a vision to life suddenly present themselves in ways that we could never plan for. Or our past experience in completely unrelated sectors somehow comes into play, giving us the precise skills and knowledge we need to navigate a situation. It has been an incredible experience to go through, and one that has filled us to the brim with faith and belief—and then reaffirmed that faith and belief time and time again. Our job in all of this seems to be to listen and to believe, both in ourselves and in the spirits that are guiding and looking out for us.

With the passage of time, we've come to realize that all of those seemingly random people who came into the store asking for crystals were really messengers, sent to us by spirit. They were like breadcrumbs leading us to a trail but, at the time, we couldn't see the landscape. Still, spirit kept on trying and trying until finally, we got it. Spirit is always talking, always sending signs, but sometimes it takes us humans a while to pay attention and get it. All of this is just as true in your life as it is in ours. We just know to be on the lookout for it now.

Although we've become more business savvy over the years, to some extent, we continue to run HOI under the direction of spirit. We've learned to never discount any idea that someone proposes to us, no matter how random it might initially appear to be. Instead, we ask spirit to have another person bring us the same message again if it's something they want us to take action on. This happens a lot, but it continues to feel magical every single time. Learning to trust these messages—both the ones that come from our own intuition and those that come from others—has been a journey. We have learned to accept the fact that intuition and messages don't always follow a linear path. Whenever we follow our intuition, it's always leading us somewhere that we're meant to go, even though the journey doesn't always follow a straight line. Over the years, we've learned the same lesson we learned in the seeming disintegration of each of our personal and professional lives and the evolution of House of Intuition: that a big part of practicing magic is engaging in an ongoing process of letting expectation go. Of course this isn't always easy.

Today, the HOI stores look almost unrecognizable from that first one in Echo Park. Gone are the days of gold spray paint. Today, our stores have a crisp, clean, open, black-and-white aesthetic. They are designed to be inviting, unintimidating, and very neutral, but, to us, using black and white symbolizes the light and shadow inside of us; we all have spirit and we all have ego. We're all human. HOI stores are intentionally non-witchy in appearance, because we want *everyone* to feel comfortable walking through our door. Magic is not just for Wiccans or hippies or New Age junkies—every last one of us can benefit from it. While our clientele certainly includes its fair share of seasoned magic practitioners, we also see people who have never considered themselves to be so much as even open to magic wander into our stores every day. Those customers are the most fun. It's amazing to watch people realize what magic *really* is and, from there, to become intrigued by and open to the idea. After all, anyone can burn a candle or light some incense.

Our only intention for House of Intuition was to have a little corner of the world to call our own, a place that stood for what we believed in. We never intended to grow beyond that first store. We never intended to bring crystals into it or any of our own magic or rituals, which we'll get into later. We certainly never planned to have the ten stores we do today or an international reach. Apparently, spirit had a plan much bigger than our own. We handle the logistics and mechanics of HOI, but we are not the creators. We just listen as spirit works through us. The world needs more of this right now.

While our story is unlikely in so many ways, in others it makes perfect sense. Everything we went through up until we met each other and created HOI led us to this point. Our religious background connected us with the notion of something bigger than ourselves from a young age. Our break with religion allowed us to open our minds and become seekers. Marlene's business experience armed us with the tools we needed to make good business decisions, even if we never really meant to apply those lessons to a magic shop. Being stripped of everything material showed us what unconditional love really looks like. And there were so many lessons in forgiveness, release, and surrender along the way. Even the hardest parts of our story, like Marlene's failed marriage and Alex's mom's brain tumor, now seem like parts of a pact we made before we came here. All of these really difficult circumstances forced us to evolve. In fact, today Marlene feels grateful to her sister for providing the opening and opportunity to meet Alex, to build this life that would have never happened otherwise (believe it or not, her sister even works at HOI now). You can probably see stories like this in your own life.

Looking back, it feels like we were being molded to get here all along. Your story might very well be the same—it is for so many of us. The lessons we learn, the times that feel so hard as we are going through them, are actually preparing us for and leading us to our destiny. Even though it might not feel like that in the moment.

The House of Intuition was born through a lot of hurt, pain, and struggle. And it was also born from magic.

PART TWO

MAGIC 101

CHAPTER THREE

IT'S NOT WITCHY

AT AN EARLIER POINT IN OUR LIVES, THERE'S NO WAY EITHER OF US WOULD'VE BE-lieved that we would one day own a magic shop. We wouldn't even know what the hell you were talking about. *What is magic?* To us, it was something "other" people did—and definitely not the type of people we wanted to hang out with. People who were weird and witchy, and who liked to hang out in dark, musty spaces, messing around with forces that weren't meant to be messed with.

Today, we think of magic as the opposite of all of those things. Magic is light and natural, just like us, because we humans are made for magic. We are meant to grow, to heal ourselves, to be intuitive, to feel empowered, and to be in touch with forces larger than ourselves. At the end of the day, magic is both a path to and a practice of all of these things. In fact, we would go so far as to say that magic is innate to all of us, even though it's trained out of most of us in Western culture at some point in our lives. Magic becomes harder to access when we feel small, disconnected, or are told that we shouldn't believe. The beauty of magic is that, when we discover it (or, more accurately, *rediscover* it), we live in a renewed state of awareness that we are powerful, connected, and that there is every reason to have faith in something bigger than ourselves. As you will soon see, the more you invite magic into your life, the more aligned you will become with yourself, with your purpose, and with the world around you.

Most important, magic is not something that exists outside of ourselves. Sure, there are tools we can use to more easily access what naturally exists within us (and we'll talk about them extensively in the pages to come), but all they are, are tools. You don't need superpowers or an extraordinary lineage to get in touch with your magic. To be honest, you don't even need this book, although it might inspire or guide you toward the first steps of creating a magical practice. It is *practice* that's really at the heart of magic. It's through practice that we access the gifts within.

Over the years, we've come under fire for these beliefs by some who practice more established or tribal magic. There are certain groups who believe that magic does have to be done a certain way or that we are co-opting belief systems that belong to a certain type of religious practice. Our point of view has always been that as human beings we all have one thing in common: We are spirits living on this earth, having a human experience. As spirits, we all have gifts that we can access in whatever way feels true to us. If the way we do that doesn't have a long lineage or include recipes handed down by wizards and warlocks—well, that's okay. The two of us and the thousands of clients we have worked with and heard stories from over the years are a testament that intuition and magic are a natural birthright, and that the practice of those things can look any number of different ways. For us, that practice involves the gifts of Mother Earth and all of the natural resources (both internal and external) that were put here for us to enjoy.

We've met plenty of people who fear that delving into magic "unattended" will open up the door to some sort of dark portal. (Ouija boards, anyone?) Marlene thought the same. But that's impossible, simply because you're already holding the magic inside of you. *You* are the magic and you are the key to unlocking your own magic. You don't need a guide or a guru or any sort of supervision—and if anyone tells you differently, we suggest you run in the other direction as quickly as you can.

The kind of magic we're talking about here can impact the way you lead your life on a day-to-day basis. All of us are in a constant conversation with our spirits and the universe, but many people don't realize it, and so the conversation is one-way. A frustrating monologue that spirit is having with you, wondering when you are going to stop and listen, to talk back to them.

Ritual (in other words, the practice of magic) is a way of cultivating and harnessing that communication. Once you do this, you will realize how powerful your connection to spirit is. The impact of that realization will trickle out into every single facet of your life. We're talking about *everything*, right down to the way you talk, because once you realize how much power you hold and how quickly the universe responds to the words you say (and even the thoughts you think), you'll become much more aware of what you're putting out there.

We've all experienced the power of our own thoughts and words before. Does this scenario ring a bell? You recently broke up with someone and, in a conversation with your girlfriend, you say something like, "Ugh, I can't believe I was ever with that guy. Thank God it's over. I wonder what he's doing now?" Then, lo and behold! You go to Trader Joe's the next day, and who should you see but your ex-boyfriend?

Well, of *course* you see your ex, because you just called him in with the power of your words and intentions. We can all relate to these "coincidences," but they're more than that. They are visible affirmation of our power and magic. They are the results of our communication with the universe and what we're calling in through that communication. As we see it, the practice of magic is all about being intentional with that conversation and power. It's about being thoughtful about what we put out there, so that we create a life in which we're drawing what we want and need to us, rather than haphazardly wielding our power in ways that don't serve us.

Once you begin practicing magic, you'll start to experience an entirely different type of alignment than you know today. You'll act in more positive ways—even when you don't want to and when no one is looking. You'll walk your talk. The messages that you're already receiving will suddenly become clearer. You'll begin to find your purpose and realize that your purpose equally wants to find you.

In this discussion of magic, it's also important to mention fear. Some people begin practicing magic because they *think* they want change, but then discover they're not actually prepared for change when it arrives. They haven't done the work. We see this all the time when, for instance, someone comes into HOI and buys a Road Opener candle because they want a new job. They go home, light the candle, and perform the ritual. Then they're surprised when they lose that job they never liked in the first place a few weeks later. They're confused because *that's* not how they imagined things happening!

Situations like this happen when we want change, but also want to control what that change looks like based on fear of the unknown. We want to simultaneously hold on and move on. The truth is, we don't control how the universe gives us what we ask for. Marlene certainly didn't want to attain love, abundance, and purpose by losing everything and having her heart broken into smithereens. And Alex didn't want to experience the fear of losing her mother and her livelihood on the road to finding community, empowerment, love, and affluence.

Truly embracing magic requires us to let go of our specific visions for how things "should" happen and to instead accept the fact that we are working in tandem with the wisdom of the universe. That process is not always as easy as we might want it to be. Magic or not, the universe still requires us to do the work, and it doesn't have the same regard for our comfort zone that we do. The universe doesn't like stagnation, because it wants us to grow and become the best, most fully realized version of ourselves. Like it or not, the reality is that growth and discomfort often go hand in hand. So, know that your magic will make things move on your behalf—ready or not—and try to release as much fear as you can while nature takes its course.

One last thing to know: The universe wants this growth and self-realization for you, whether you actively ask for it or not. If you're not willing to address the situations that need your attention or to ask for more, after a while the universe will take action on your behalf. Both of our lives are a testament to this. We were both clinging on to the status quo in different ways, despite all of the signs that it wasn't working, that there was something more out there for us. Finally, the universe decided enough was enough.

So, really think about it: Do you want the changes that are necessary in your life to be your choice? Or do you want them to be like the rug that gets pulled out from under your feet, resulting in a face-plant before you stagger back up onto your feet and carry on once again?

The bottom line is this: You *are* the magic. Once you begin to realize this, everything changes. When we all begin to realize this as a society, things will change in an incredibly profound and beautiful way. One of the things that we see as so powerful in the younger generations is that, unlike the older ones who often have stories like ours of having the rug pulled out from under them before finding a spiritual practice, the young ones are out there actively seeking before this happens. This will be a very exciting evolution to witness, and we're grateful to be here for it.

ARE YOU WITCHES?

Obviously, we are not witches in the black-hat, broom-toting kind of way. But under the technical definition of *witch*—one who creates magic—then, sure we are! And so are you, because you hold magic within, too. We all do.

It's been interesting to watch the connotation of the word *witch* shift away from darkness and fear, even in the relatively short span of time that HOI has been around. Witches have had a bad rap for a long time, and only in the past several years have they come to be considered cool. This is largely a millennial thing, and we are grateful to see the shift occur.

MAGIC AND RELIGION

MAGIC IS NOT RELIGIOUS OR SPIRITUAL IN AND OF ITSELF, BUT DISCOVERING AND practicing magic *can* be a spiritual process, and it can certainly make you look at the forces around you in a different way. It can act as a gateway to understanding that there is something more out there. What that something more is, though, is up to you, because magic—or at least the type of magic we'll discuss in this book—is separate from any organized sort of belief. Much more important than what you believe in is that you learn to believe in yourself.

While neither of us practices a specific religion anymore, we do still enjoy certain religious environments, and sometimes go to church with our mothers to soak the environment in. For us, religion established a good foundation of faith and helped us in many ways. We even continue to incorporate some Catholic prayers and figures into our magical rituals because they resonate with us.

While magic and religion are separate, they can be complementary; it's not a one-or-the-other type of situation. There is no set "God" in magic. You can make offerings to whichever entity feels appropriate to you, or perhaps to no specific entity whatsoever (for example, you might dedicate your offerings to nature or the divine knowing of the universe). What matters is tapping into your own intuition and what feels right to you and your set of beliefs.

Magic is very different from religion insofar as religion tends to provide a set of rules and a list of dos and don'ts. Magic is the opposite. Part of the beauty of magic and ritual is that you create your own road map—and you rely on your own intuition and inner compass to do so. Magic and the spirituality that is embedded within it will help you navigate life.

Our spiritual practice, which includes but is not limited to magic, has allowed us to get *closer* to God. Now instead of feeling like we have to go to church to acknowledge or communicate with God, we just walk down the hallway to our altar and pray there. Our spirituality is with us all the time, a part of our everyday lives.

While magic is not a religion, like religion, magic requires faith. Faith in yourself and in the universe. Magic asks us to turn our faith inward, to believe in our own power and innate knowing. Simultaneously, magic asks us to have faith in the fact that the universe is kind and has our best interests at heart. It's up to us to recognize and put our intentions out there in the way that feels most intuitively natural, but then we have to sit back and wait for the universe to respond, knowing that it will do so with everyone's highest good in mind. It's for this reason that we always advise people to wait at least twenty-one days before performing a ritual for the same intention over again. (Optimally, they will wait three months, and there are certain instances in which a spell should only be done once.) For example, perhaps you light a candle to promote opened communication with a friend you used to be close to, but are now experiencing conflict with. You wait it out, do the work on your part, and, still, the lines of communication remain closed. By continuing to repeat this ritual that involves not only you, but also another person's free will and best interests, you are trying to control another person's behavior. The bottom line is that not all of our intentions *should* be manifested—or at least not in the way we think. Put it out there, have faith that the universe hears you, and allow it to respond in kind.

DABBLING IN THE DARK

Every now and then, people come to us and ask for certain things that aren't in the greatest good of all. For example, perhaps they are in love with a married man and want to know if there are any magical rituals that might convince their boyfriend to leave his wife.

These requests tend to come from people who have established some sort of magical practice and have already seen firsthand how quickly things can happen and shifts can occur. When we encounter cases like this, we remind the person that our thoughts and actions (and, thus, our magic) are like a boomerang. Whatever you send out is going to come back and hit you. Dealing in magic that is not in the highest good or that attempts to take power from others is like writing out a big, fat check that you are going to have to pay at some point down the line.

Along with this, we have to give the universe time to do its work. This requires faith in the fact that, even if you can't see things happening the way you want them to or think they should, the universe has heard you and is churning away in the background, working on your behalf. In addition to having faith in the universe, you also have to have faith in yourself, in your power, and in your magic. When people repeat the same spell or ritual over and over again, what they're really saying is that they don't have faith or trust in the universe for having their best interests in mind or in the power of the magic that came from within.

ARE HEXES AND CURSES FOR REAL?

In this world, there is both dark energy and light, just like we all carry shadow and light within ourselves. Yes, even you. But we believe that the energy of love and light is stronger than dark energies. Ultimately, the light will win every time over the long run.

Having said this, dark energy doesn't naturally translate to hexes or curses, which are something we get asked about a lot. In our experience, hexes and curses might exist, but *both* parties have to buy into them, including the person who the spell is cast upon. If someone believes in and puts a lot of energy into the idea that they have a hex or curse on them, they are giving their power away. Remember, when we speak (or think), the universe responds.

Most of us will not be impacted by hexes or curses, though. More often than not, people buy into the fact that they've been hexed or cursed when it offers the easiest explanation for the things that are—or are not—happening in their lives. It's a way out of the work. It's easier to blame a hex for the fact that your love life constantly falls apart than it is to look within and figure out which behaviors or beliefs might be getting in your own way. It's easier than taking accountability for your own reality.

When people come into HOI worried that they have a curse on them, we refocus and redirect their energy to what's going on in their lives. What are they doing? Where are they at in their life? We break the "curse" down in a logical way and help them understand that the answer is almost always personal work and growth. Not curse removal. We also point out that if the person in front of us believes that curses have power, they must also believe that their spirit guides, guardian angels, and ancestors have power. So where are their protectors in all of this? Did they just take a vacation day?

Remember, *you* have all the control and the power over your life and future.

MAGIC IS AVAILABLE TO ALL OF US

LOTS OF PEOPLE MAKE A GREAT LIVING OFF OF THE NOTION THAT MAGIC IS SOME-thing that's only available to a specific subset of people. We've had so many customers walk into our store or contact us online over the years with stories that go something like this: I was told that I have a curse on me and that I have to pay $1,500 to a spiritual practitioner to have it removed. *No. No, no, no.* If you ever hear something like this, recognize it as a waving red flag and move on.

In our experience, there are stages to both spirituality and a magical practice. People who end up turning to magic usually start out feeling lost in life. They know they crave something more, but don't understand exactly what that means or how to get there. So they seek the guidance of someone else. It's at this point that people often stumble into HOI, often not even understanding exactly why they've come. It's why Marlene arrived at the tarot reader's shop and how Alex found herself at the religious ceremony. Through experiences like this, many of those seekers experience the incredible revelation that there is something more out there. This might look any number of ways: They could get an uncanny reading that involves a deceased loved one or they might start to notice synchronicities in their lives that seem to carry within them some sort of greater meaning. These initial experiences and revelations are sort of like a gateway drug. They often make people want to feel and learn more, to see what this—whatever "this" is—is all about. At this initial point, most people believe they need outside guidance to access greater forces.

After receiving some guidance or having enough of these "something more" experiences, a greater curiosity is sparked and the desire to learn creeps in. This often shows up as a calling to incorporate some sort of personal practice that is not reliant on others into their lives. We love it when we meet people who are in this phase, because it's the first important step toward living a life in magic, toward spiritual independence. And *that's* where the tools and rituals we'll talk about in this book usually come in. Some people's magical practice might be as simple as prayers. For others, it might include things like ritual, working with the cycles of the moon, candles, herbs, oils, or incense. It could also consist of something altogether different from any of this if your intuition points you in that direction.

Regardless of what this magical practice looks like, once it's in place, people usually come to realize that they can begin to build a temple in their own home. They discover they are not reliant on anyone, anywhere, or anything to connect. The power lies within. It's just a matter of learning, practicing, and cultivating trust in yourself.

It is our mission to point people toward the tools that can help them get to this place because, as we have learned in our own lives and seen all too often in others, people who don't have their own magical practice are not as connected to their own power or that "something more" as they could be. They don't grasp that life is not just happening to them, but that they have the power to move in the direction they want to—no settling required! Also, without developing their own practice, seekers become vulnerable to others by becoming reliant upon what they see as a practice that only "extraordinary" people have access to. In reality, we are *all* extraordinary.

INTUITION

INTUITION IS NOT MAGIC, BUT THE RESULTS OF IT CAN BE. INTUITION PLAYS A KEY role in our magical practice, as it can in all other facets of life. Intuition gives us insight, and the more insight we recognize and put into practice, the better off we are. You can think of intuition as your GPS to the material world.

Intuition is built into each and every one of us, whether we recognize it or not. You've felt your intuition at play before, even if you haven't called it that. For some people, intuition is a sensation in their stomach; for others it might be a ringing in their ear. Intuition presents itself as any number of feelings or sensations, and it's different for each of us. Even if we press our intuition down or don't acknowledge it, in some way we all recognize intuition for what it is, even if only subconsciously.

We get to choose whether we tune in to our intuition or tune it out. When we make the choice to ignore it, we often find ourselves in sticky situations that we could have avoided. For example, you might know that someone's energy doesn't feel quite right to you the very first time you meet them, but press ahead with a friendship anyway. When it all gets messy and falls apart a couple of years later, you look back and think, "I *knew* that. I *knew* how this was going to end before it even began. Why didn't I listen to myself?" In all fairness, society trains us not to listen to our intuition; we are a society that places logic above all else. But if you watch a baby or a little kid, it's easy to see how in touch with their intuition they are. Until they're told intuition is somehow wrong or not real, that is. Which is why so many adults find themselves trying to tune back in to this thing that is innate to us.

Intuition is intangible, but the two of us view it as concrete information that is downloaded from the spirit world. So, when it comes to the interplay of intuition and magic, your intuition often provides you with information that your guides want you to put into practice to bring your intentions to fruition. It's for this reason that we all have to be active participants in our own magic. No one else's intuition can tell you what *you* are supposed to do. You are in full possession of your own unique creative power and only you can access it fully. Learning to trust this intuition is like working out a muscle you haven't used in a long time. When we get to the rituals section of this book (see page 117), we're going to give you lots of opportunities to put your own intuition into practice so that you can experience for yourself how uncannily accurate your intuition really is.

Obviously, the two of us love getting tarot readings, and have received a lot of guidance from them. In the early days of HOI, it felt very important for us to make this same experience available to others. But as the early years of the shop went by, we began to realize that the same people were booking appointments again and again, with just a short span of time in between. It became apparent that some of our clients were outsourcing their decisions to readers or asking the same question over and over again until they received the answer they wanted to hear.

Yes, this meant more income for the store, but it felt wrong to us—almost like we were inadvertently preying upon vulnerable people. That was the *last* thing we wanted to do. We began putting holds on clients between readings to give people time to make their own decisions, establish new habits and practices, and allow situations to play themselves out. Basically, we attempted to enforce the idea that customers had to do their own work. Some customers understood this and others did not. They argued that it was their money and they had the right to spend it however they wanted. "Absolutely," we would respond. "But it's our shop, and we are not being of service to you if we're just taking your money." We didn't want to bear the karma of that.

It started to feel important to us to create a way for clients to learn to recognize and utilize their own intuition and magic. After all, the healers that our clients were leaning on are just as human as anyone else, even if the work they do can feel extraordinary at times. Really, readers and healers are just messengers who have their own stuff to work on, too. Over the years, we've had a lot of incredible healers at HOI, but we've also seen a few whose egos have become wrapped up in their practice; they've bought into their own hype. Of course, it can be difficult for healers to stay in a servant mindset when they are being praised for changing lives on a daily basis. In some cases, a certain type of celebrity status can be bestowed on healers. It's important that healers understand how to balance the sense of power that can come from this. Otherwise, it's not good for anyone involved. Healers who are stuck in a place of ego are never going to be able to teach clients how to tap into and rely on their own intuition. To us, that's the most important function for a healer to serve.

As time went on at HOI, we saw that people were leaning on us too much. They wanted us to tell them how to communicate and interact with spirit and magic. Certainly, others can act as guides, but so much of this is DIY work. As time went on, we began to wonder if, despite our best intentions, we were actually disempowering people. Were we really helping our clients if they weren't learning?

We decided the answer was no.

Once we had this realization, HOI became much less about readings and much more about teaching, beginning with meditation.

As our understanding of our own magic and power grew, it became clearer and clearer to us that what we really wanted to do at HOI was teach people how to dig deep and listen to themselves, just as we had learned to listen to ourselves over the years. We wanted to give people what they needed to do their own work, rather than doing it for them and disempowering them in the process. It's not helpful to give people answers if they don't have the tools to work with those answers. We began bringing on teachers rather than healers so that our community had access to a wide variety of tools, including meditation, astrology, oils, and candle magic. Today, classes like this are pretty common, but when we started this program in 2013, they weren't. The people who did teach these sorts of practices were usually also the type of people who didn't so much as own a television. They certainly didn't have a platform to get the word out about what they were teaching in any sort of significant way. HOI was able to provide that for them.

Strengthening the intuition muscle takes a combination of patience, trust, and gratitude. We are proof of this. Neither of us grew up seeing dead people (although Marlene felt them as a child, without really understanding what was happening) or channeling the future. But we spent enough time at the spiritual gym that our intuition began to seep through in our daily lives. For example, Marlene discovered that she could channel energies, see people's ancestors, or that words that turned out to be meaningful appeared before her as if they were flying on a banner. Alex came to have an intuitive understanding of how magic worked, especially when it comes to cleansing. She's always got a broom with her in our house or the shop, and she does the same thing figuratively through the energetic cleansing of spaces, which we'll teach you how to do in the Rituals section. We sure as hell know we're not superhuman, so accessing our own intuitive powers taught us once and for all that each of us has access to intuition in its various forms. It just takes more practice for some people than for others.

As part of all of our classes, we're constantly teaching our clients that expectations can be the death of intuition. You have to get to the point where you are willing to allow a tapestry to be woven. To see how the different messages you receive may not directly result in exactly what you were hoping for immediately, but that they are all leading somewhere over the long run. Spirit talks for a reason, and helps guide us through the different steps we are meant to take along this journey.

Take this, for instance: Let's say that the two of us feel guided to create a money jar and build a ritual around that. We create our jar and then wait for the money to roll in—but it doesn't. That doesn't mean our magic didn't work or that our intuition was misguided. Perhaps we were guided to create that money jar because we will eventually need a cash infusion farther down the line. When that moment comes, we'll be ready to roll. Or maybe someone will cross our path who needs a money jar. It could also be that we just needed to learn something in the process of creating that jar that will go on to benefit us in any number of ways. It might be that working on that magic draws the two of us closer together in a time when we need it. There are any number of outcomes to these scenarios, and you have to allow them to play out, and to trust your intuition in the meantime—even in those moments when it feels like it may have led you in the wrong direction.

We have learned to always be grateful to spirit for communicating with us, even when we don't understand what the point of its message was. One thing that has become abundantly clear to us over the years, through both our own experiences and those others have shared with us, is that spirit is always working to our benefit. Even when we can't see it right away.

Once you begin to trust in your own intuition you can more easily stay on the right path. When negativity comes your way, you will be able to identify it and extract the lessons necessary more quickly and easily. Intuition serves as a great source of peace and harmony that is generated from within. It allows us to release fear because the more in touch with our intuition we become, the more we understand how powerful we really are.

INTENTION

INTENTION WORKS IN TANDEM WITH INTUITION TO ESTABLISH THE FOUNDATION FOR magic. At the heart of every ritual or magical practice you undertake should be intention, or things you want to bring into your life and into the world.

Here's the weird thing about intention, though. Human beings have a tendency to be flighty. When you're able to really focus on your intentions, they can be incredibly powerful. In fact, intentions are magical in and of themselves. Take Carol, one of our HOI managers, for instance. When she was a freshman in high school, a sophomore caught her eye. Not once did she speak to him, but she saw him every day. And, every day, she pointed him out to her friends at lunchtime and said, "There goes my boyfriend." Calling this guy her boyfriend became a running joke for Carol and her circle.

Three years passed and, still, Carol and her "boyfriend" never once spoke, but the joke remained.

It wasn't until Carol was a senior that, out of the blue, her "boyfriend" liked one of her pictures on Facebook. Carol liked one of his back. The two of them started to DM, which turned into texting, which turned into a full-blown relationship that's still going strong eight years later.

Without even understanding what she was doing at the time, Carol put a strong, consistent, specific intention out into the universe, and the universe responded, as it does.

Which leads us to the next point: Specificity is *important.* Another one of our employees, Ryan, lit a Love Fix candle following a breakup with his boyfriend. This breakup happened before Ryan worked at HOI, so we hadn't yet had the opportunity to drill the importance of specificity into his head. Ryan lit the candle and set the intention to "bring him back." Unfortunately, Ryan didn't specify who "him" was.

Later that night, *another* ex reached out to Ryan, asking if he was free to hang out. Ryan sent the signal out to the universe and an ex responded—just not the ex that Ryan had intended. (By the way, Ryan said yes to the other ex's offer, and a couple of fun weeks ensued before Ryan got his most recent ex out of his system. Today, Ryan is always sure to remind our clients about how important it is to be specific in their intentions. The universe *is* listening, so be mindful about what you are (and aren't) saying.

To help our clients stay focused and specific in their intentions, we embed crystals into the bottom of our candles. Not only do these crystals infuse the candles with more power, but they also provide people with a lasting reminder of the intentions they have set and rituals they have performed over time. Generally speaking, whenever you practice magic or perform a ritual, it's always a good idea to utilize something tangible that you can keep with you until that ritual comes to fruition. This will serve as a constant reminder to remain present with your intention. It's why practices like vision boarding and journaling are so powerful—they offer us an opportunity to look back and reflect; to remind us where we've been and where we want to go. These reminders keep us focused, and they are a big part of the success of spells and rituals. Momentary intention is not enough to effect change; focus and consistency in our intentions are key. While magic allows you to call upon and enlist the help of sources greater than yourself, you are ultimately co-creating with them. Without focused intention, you are asking spirit to do all the work. Spirit isn't really down with that because, after all, the entire purpose of this human life is to grow and to learn. You have to do the work; spirit is here just to support and guide you when necessary.

Generally, rituals are thought of as happening in a short span of time. And, sure, some of them can be pretty speedy. For example, if you are saging your house as part of a cleansing ritual, chances are that you will complete that ritual in a few minutes' time. But rituals can also extend over long expanses of time—days, weeks, or even years—and they can look any number of ways. Marlene is a prime example of this. She's been in a state of ritual since 2018, and no one would ever know it from the outside. For Christmas that year, Marlene's mom gave her a necklace with a heart-shaped charm on it. Marlene took the charm to her altar and sat with it, setting the intention to communicate better with and love her mom unconditionally. She wears the necklace every single day as a constant reminder of her intention and what she's working on. It's a reminder to be present with and focused on that intention. It's a reminder to do the work, to remain focused on spiritual growth and all of the ways it trickles out into daily life and interactions.

Follow-through has a lot to do with the success of our spells, and that follow-through is dependent upon the strength and continued focus on intention. Keeping our intentions close to the front of our minds brings a potent dose of energy to our magic.

One final thing to think about here is that, although we often don't think of it this way, gratitude is also a form of intention—and it's a powerful one. When we look at our lives through the lens of awareness and gratitude, we are sending out into the universe a powerful beacon that draws more of what we want and love our way. We remain in a constant state of communicating our thanks to spirit, and keeping our focus on what *is* working, rather than what's not.

CHAPTER FOUR

THE POTION ROOM

ALL OF THIS SOUNDS GREAT, BUT MAGIC STILL CAN BE A VERY NEBULOUS IDEA WHEN you're new to it. To help you along your magical path, we're going to share some of the tools, ingredients, and practices that we most like to use in our magical work. All of these are things that can be found in our Potion Room—this is the place where we make and infuse all of our stores' products. Many people assume that, as HOI has grown, we've outsourced the creation of our various candles, oils, scrubs, and so on. This couldn't be farther from the truth. While we *do* have a bigger team these days, every item we offer to our customers is intentionally infused with the sacred energy and intention we want to help bring in. Our Potion Room is the place where we do this and, among other tools you'll read about in this chapter, there is an altar right at the center of this room.

Don't worry, you're not going to read about birds' blood, cats' whiskers, or even magic wands here. This is all really normal stuff, some of which you may very well already have on hand. If you don't, you can find almost all of these items easily or at a low cost. Throughout the remainder of this book, we'll explain how to use these everyday items in a ritualistic way.

One last thought before you get started: Don't go rushing out to buy all of these materials in bulk or advance to have on hand for magic you *might* want to do in the future. You can take your intuition out for a spin by allowing the right ritual to find you at the right time, and being in the moment as you prepare for it. (And, by the way, preparation is part of the ritual—but more on that later.)

THE BASICS

ALTAR

At the center of almost all of the magic we do is our altar. We consider it our switchboard that provides a direct line to all the spiritual entities that assist us on a regular basis. That switchboard is always on.

Creating an altar in your home will serve as a constant reminder of your intentions, your faith in something greater working on your behalf, and your faith in yourself. It will provide you with an easy way to tune in to and communicate with the energies surrounding you so that you can navigate life with the help of their energy and guidance.

Is an altar necessary to communicate with these spirits? Of course not. But it *does* serve as a powerful reminder to keep those channels open to facilitate a constant connection to spirit and those you have lost. Every time you pass your altar, you will be reminded of the powerful energies that surround you and that are at play in your life. The importance of this communication can't be overstated. It's just like with the people in your life in the material world. If you are ignoring or not paying attention to them, after a while they're not going to make as much of an effort to communicate. The same goes for spirit.

Altars can also be a space of comfort. You can go to the altar when you feel alone or need to find a sense of tranquility or a reminder that everything is going to be okay, no matter what is happening in your life or how much things might feel like they are falling apart. It's a place to go when you need to release your worries or even just to have a good cry.

All the reasons why people might go to church? You can also go to your altar for those reasons (and, of course, you can go to church, too). The beauty of having an altar is that you never have to leave your house or feel like you have to wait for a certain time to communicate, celebrate, or pray. The altar will always be there waiting for you at any time of day. You can connect with spirit at any moment, even on the craziest days, and even in your pajamas.

CANDLES

Long before there was HOI and before we even really understood what we were doing, there were candles. They've been at the center of our magical practice for a long time, as they have been for so many others for thousands of years before us. To this day, candles continue to be one of our favorite tools because they are incredibly powerful, while also simple to use. Candles are a great entry into ritual and magic because they are unintimidating and relatable to pretty much all of us.

One of the reasons candles are so powerful is because they hold within them all four elements. In solid form, they relate to the earth; when they are burned down, they transform into liquid, which is symbolic of water; the flame represents fire; and candles require air to burn. Embedded crystals bring even more of the earth element in, and also amplify the power of the candles and the intentions they symbolize (more on the amplification power of crystals on page 249).

Many people sense there is something mystical, powerful, or energetic about candles. Think about it: How many times have you lit a candle of a certain scent or color with the intention of setting a specific type of vibe? It's one of those things human beings do, without giving much thought as to *why*.

In the early days of HOI, we weren't selling candles, but we frequently made candles for our regulars. Someone might tell us, for example, that they needed a new job, so we would infuse a candle on their behalf. To do this, we prepared the candle for ritual by rubbing symbolic herbs and oils into the top of the candle, put it on our altar to pray over for a few days, and then brought it to that person with instructions about how to burn the candle in a ritualistic way. The instructions were different for every person and issue. In the example of finding a new job, we might give that person an orange candle to light on Monday and leave burning for three days.

Every time we did this, the person we gifted the candle to insisted on paying us. We always refused because it felt wrong to put a price on spirituality. (And, simultaneously, we wondered why HOI was failing.) Nonetheless, people started to donate money of their own accord, often telling us that if we wouldn't take the money, they wanted us to put it toward the supplies necessary to pay it forward to the next person who came to us for assistance. As we began to move away from providing readings to focus on magic and ritualistic products, candles were the first proof to us that people were *definitely* interested in something beyond readers and healers.

In the beginning, the two of us held each and every candle in our hands as we meditated over it, then placed the candles by our altar for several weeks to infuse them with prayer. After that time had passed, we came back to the altar and, with a journal in hand, asked spirit what candles we could bring into the world that would assist people in bringing in their highest good. Every time, we got a number of words, such as *forgiveness, gratitude, love,* and *self-love.* As each word came in, we sat with it, then asked our spirits what oils they would like infused in the candle to facilitate the intention. By the time we were done, we might have dozens of words and recipes.

We often received messages from the spirits about oils that we weren't familiar with so, when we finished meditating and downloading information, only then would we cross-check what the oils symbolized. It blew our mind—it still does!—because, without fail, everything was right on point. For example, we might channel bergamot oil for a candle intended to bring in stability, only to find out that bergamot symbolizes success and can restore stability. It was a powerful practice. We then put each of the oils we were told to use on our altar and prayed over them, channeling intentions into them. Then we infused the oils—and, thus, intention—into the candles, and placed crystals in the bottom of the candle so that people could keep the crystals with them long after the candle burned all the way down, to remind them of their intention. Once the candles were made, we put them on the shelf at HOI with just a single word of description, such as *creativity.*

Despite how much we've grown since our first foray into candles, our process is still exactly the same as it was from the very beginning. Our altar is just much larger now, and so are our batches.

WHEN CUSTOMERS PURCHASE a candle, we teach them how to properly burn it. You will burn your ritualistic candles the same way: Place the candle in a bowl of water, which simultaneously serves as a safety mechanism and represents emotion and flow, then light it. Set your intention for the outcome you desire, then visualize that outcome as you meditate over the burning candle. Watching a magic candle burn is a pretty cool experience. If you notice, most candles have a steady flame, but a magic candle often has a tall flame, flickers, dances, or even crackles.

Candle magic is powerful for a few reasons, one of which is that candles offer a ritual that lasts for an extended period of time—every time the candle burns, you are reminded of the intention you have set. You may very well burn your candle several times in the course of a single ritual. When you are ready to extinguish the flame, you will want to snuff it out rather than blow it out because you don't want to symbolically blow out your intention. Our breath is more powerful than we give it credit for; after all, breath gives us life. You can purchase a snuffer to extinguish your candle. A plate works just as well to put out candles that are contained in glass holders.

When performing candle magic, you'll want to consider the color that symbolizes your intention. (For more on color symbolism see page 111, or use your own intuition for guidance.) Candle magic can be enhanced and specified by infusing your candle with herbs or oils, just like we do with the candles we sell in the shop. For example, if you are doing a candle ritual for money, you might select a green candle and add in a pinch of cinnamon. Green candles represent money and abundance, while cinnamon is known to bring in money and will amplify the power of your ritual. Note that *pinch* is the keyword when adding herbs—in candle magic, less is always more because we are working with flame. You can add oils, too, and this is known as the process of anointing. Like herbs, oils should be used sparingly. Tilt the bottle of essential oil onto your fingertip, then rub your fingertip around the top of the candle, into the wax. If you want to bring something into your life, rub the oil clockwise; to reverse or release something or for protection from something, rub the oil counterclockwise.

Every time you relight your candle, you begin your ritual anew. This means you will want to reset and visualize your intention with each lighting. Continue doing this until the candle has completely burned down. When we finish a candle, we like to keep the candleholder as a reminder. Sometimes we use them as vases; other times, we incorporate them into our altar and place crystals or other offerings inside of them. This can be a great way to invoke symbolism. For example, if you are doing a money spell, you might keep the candle container on your altar and fill it with coins or money. It's also okay to recycle or dispose of your candleholders, but be thoughtful about how and where you do so because this intention-infused object is now sacred. The container continues to hold the vibration of your intention's energy. For example, if you are doing a healing ritual, dispose of your candle in a recycling bin at a hospital or healing center; if you are doing a money ritual, do the same at a bank. This same strategy can be applied to any offerings you may place on your altar, but later want to dispose of.

CRYSTALS

Crystals play a big role in our story and, over the years, have become one of our favorite go-to magical tools. Today, we have crystals for various purposes all around our house, our stores, and often even in our pocket or purse. We even keep crystals in our dogs' water bowls to purify the water and infuse it with protective energy, as well as in our garden to nurture our plants.

Crystals are one of nature's great gifts to us, and have been used for various spiritual and protective purposes for thousands of years.

Because crystals are of the earth, they are pure. They connect us to and ground us in specific frequencies based on the minerals they are composed of and where they are from. Although we might possess crystals, they don't really belong to us. They are permanent (yet another reason why they are such powerful intention-setting tools), and we are merely their temporary caretakers.

Crystals conduct light, sound, and electricity and, because of this, have the ability to transform, amplify, transmit, and absorb high-intensity energy. They bring a vibration into their space, which means that when you carry a crystal with you, you bring that same vibration with you.

Getting started with crystals is simple: Begin with the ones that you gravitate to, the ones that pull you in. Do not get stuck in a maze of research or overthinking. Crystal-picking isn't a quiz situation; your work isn't being graded and there are no right or wrong answers. We advise customers *not* to select crystals by reading write-ups because the truth of the matter is that every single crystal will relate to you and your life in some way, shape, or form. And you definitely don't want to walk away from the experience a few thousand dollars in the hole.

Remember that crystals transmit energy, and you are picking up on and being drawn to their energy as part of your intuitive process. During the selection process, graze your hand over the crystals and notice what calls to you or catches your eye. This doesn't have to be a loud, holy experience that includes the skies opening up and angels singing to you. In fact, you're much likelier to experience that calling as a slight, subtle pull toward a certain crystal. Go with that, exercising your faith and psychic muscles. This selection process is yet another small step toward learning to trust your own internal guidance.

You don't need a buffet of crystals in your arsenal. Cost aside, crystals are a resource, which means we don't want to hoard them. Start small, with just one crystal at a time. It's important to see how each one uniquely and individually impacts you. Many people underestimate the impact of crystals, and you don't want to end up like Alex, nauseated by the powerful energy of your massive new crystal collection. When you start with big numbers, you can't tell what crystals you are specifically reacting to. You want to be able to feel out and acquaint yourself with your crystals and their energy one by one. Yes, certain crystals are associated with particular properties or energies, but the truth of the matter is that each one of us interacts differently with different types of crystals. Like so many other parts of this magical work, finding the crystals that work for you is a personal process.

Even if and when your crystal collection grows over time, we still recommend that you use only two or three crystals at a time. To use your crystals, infuse them with the intention you want to set—in other words, hold that intention in your mind as you concentrate on your crystal. Once you have seen that intention through (which may happen over either a shorter or longer period of time, depending upon your intention), you can then cleanse and clear the crystal. Charge it again when you're ready to set another intention.

Clearing and cleansing crystals to purify their energy is a simple process. To clear a crystal, simply concentrate on your crystal and express gratitude for the intention it has held for you. While it's a more mechanical process, cleansing is also simple. All you will need in most cases is a little bit of water to gently rub over the crystal with your fingertips. Just be aware that certain types of crystals, such as selenite, will dissolve in water over time based on their porous composition. This means that a little bit of research is required, but the vast majority of crystals can be cleansed with water. If you happen to have a crystal that cannot handle water, instead burn sage or resin over it. If you choose, you can use sage or resin to cleanse crystals that can handle water, as well. Since full moons symbolize the completion of cycles, you might want to place your crystals under the light of the full moon to release energy that has been collected within them and to infuse them with loving, nurturing energy. Finally, you might choose to bury your crystals in a shallow grave so that Mother Earth can soak up their energy, then return the crystals to you in their natural state for continued use. Use this cleansing process as another opportunity to listen to and stretch your intuitive muscles.

After cleansing your crystals, you can charge them for use again, much like you would charge a cellphone. To do this, place your crystals in the sunlight, which will further burn off any collected energy. (As with water, be aware that some crystals cannot be in the sunlight for long periods of time, so do your research.) The new moon period is a particularly powerful time for charging and amplifying the energy of your crystal, because the moon's energy is stronger and more amplified at this point in the cycle. One of our favorite practices is to place our crystals in a bowl, then put the bowl outside in the rain at nighttime, for simultaneous cleansing and recharging by Mother Earth.

INCENSE + RESIN

If you're like most people, you've probably heard of incense before—colleges may as well include a package of nag champa along with their acceptance letters. Fewer people are aware of resin.

Incense and resin are quite similar, but not the same. When it comes to using one or the other, it really boils down to the ritual at hand. In our experience, incense is better used with altar offerings and setting the mood or energy in a space. Resin is powerful in rituals that incorporate intentions or spell work.

We have been into incense since the earliest days of HOI—it was one of the only things we *did* carry initially. Not for magical or ritualistic purposes, though. Originally, we thought of incense as an aromatherapy tool, as many people do. We didn't understand how powerful certain varieties of it, such as sage, dragon's blood, and copal, can be for creating and cleansing space, not to mention any number of other purposes that range from bringing in the energies of money, love, and protection. In fact, most incense is made with intention. If you think about it, even the dollar-store varieties of incense are usually called something like Love, Joy, or Peace. This means that even when people are using incense on a casual basis, they are still receiving an intention secondhand, one that was infused into it by the makers of the incense.

As we began opening multiple storefronts, the two of us got even more into incense because we realized that the aroma set the space. Customers who were used to our Echo Park store quickly felt equally at ease in Highland Park because, while it looked different, the smell and the energy the burning incense created were familiar. The ability of incense to set a space and energy is particularly true when it comes to creating a sacred space. The scent of incense elevates the energy in a room and speaks to people's spirit, rather than their physical being. Sometimes there is an element of recall to this, too; for example, people who grew up in churches might smell a certain aroma and be reminded of formative sacred or spiritual moments from their past. For others, the scent might be more of an energetic draw. Incense is one of the most essential tools to have in your magical arsenal, precisely for the reason that it creates a sacred space.

We first learned about resin from Naha, a healer who worked at HOI. She told us it was an important product for us to carry because resin is such a powerful tool for cleansing, purifying, and bringing in spirit. If you've spent time in Christian or Catholic churches, you've probably smelled resin before.

Resins are a form of pure incense. Unlike incense, resin does not include any added herbs or synthetic oils. It generally comes in the form of little pebbles. Resin is potent and just a small amount will burn for quite a while. A few pebbles should be more than enough for a single session.

While incense is directly lit, resin is burned on a charcoal tablet placed inside a vessel. This vessel might be a ceramic bowl, or an abalone shell. Abalone shells are a popular choice to hold resin because the shells hold the energy of the ocean, which is cleansing and clearing. You can get creative with your resin vessel, with the caveat that plastic containers can't be used because the charcoal used to light the resin will burn through.

To start, sprinkle salt into the bottom of your vessel to protect it from overheating or burning under the lit charcoal. Over time, ash will drop onto the salt, and that's okay! You can allow it to build up. When you're ready to begin using your resin, use a pair of tongs to light a charcoal tablet over the flame of your stove or place the charcoal on top of the salt in your vessel and use a lighter or match to light it. The charcoal will turn a whitish color when it ignites. Place the charcoal tablet in your vessel and place your resin on top of the charcoal.

Since they are from the earth, resins carry certain vibrations with them and are used for different purposes. Note that these vibrations tend to be stronger in incense that is naturally made with herbs, essential oils, and resin mixture because they come from Mother Earth. With that in mind, also remember that the strongest element of any type of magic is ultimately the power of your intention.

- **AMBER—creates calmness; good for meditation**
- **COPAL—invites in white light and purifies; great for connecting with ancestors**
- **DRAGON'S BLOOD—exorcises and cleanses energy; good for love**
- **FRANKINCENSE—purifies and creates a sacred space**
- **MYRRH—grounds; good for meditation**

Open up your doors and windows when you use incense or resin to cleanse, in order to allow the air to move through the room and to come and go. If you are using incense (or sage, for that matter), you will begin at the back of the house and move your way toward the front. Generally speaking, the front of your house faces the outside world, whereas the back of your house leads out to more of your property. The idea is to take everything that's in your space and move it out into the world to dissipate and clear. As you move with the incense, hold your intention at the front of your mind and visualize both what you are removing from your house and what you are inviting in. Sometimes you might just be moving stagnation and replacing it with a higher vibration, just like you would remove dust from underneath the sofa or behind the tables.

USING SYNTHETIC INCENSE INTENTIONALLY

Many types of incense are made with synthetic material. If you're using synthetic incense, make sure the intention of that incense matches your own intention. You can usually verify the intention an incense is created with either in the incense title or somewhere on its packaging.

When you are using incense or resin to bring in a certain vibration such as creativity or abundance, rather than moving through the house and clearing, you will instead simply place the incense or resin in a holder and let its scent and energy roam freely and infiltrate the space. You might choose to place the holder in a specific or meaningful location that applies to what you're trying to bring in. For example, if you want to bring in more love or sexy time with your partner, perhaps you burn a love incense or resin around the bed.

HERBS AND OILS

As we get into rituals in the following section, you'll notice that most of them utilize herbs and oils. So, when we talk about magical tools, both of these are an important part of the conversation. Herbs and oils are largely interchangeable in ritual work because, after all, oils are made of herbs, so they can be used to the same effect. Long before there were pharmaceuticals, herbs were used for healing purposes and, like crystals, each type of herb carries its own frequency.

A quick note about using oils in magic: We suggest they be used sparingly. Generally, just a few drops will do. Not only are oils highly concentrated—and, thus, very potent—but, also, a lot of herbs or flowers have to be squeezed to make just a single container of essential oil. We want to be kind and respectful to Mother Earth for her offerings and to protect her resources because those resources protect us. As you'll see, none of our magic *doesn't* use the resources she provides. On a more practical note, too much oil can leave a residue on surfaces or make them slippery.

Remember that you can always add more oil to a spell, so it's best to start conservatively. The potency of the oil will vary from one container of oil to the next, even within the same brand, because each batch of oil is made from a different plant. Let your sense of smell guide you, but our general rule of thumb is to use approximately six drops of essential oil per ounce of water. If you are sensitive to smell, even one drop will do, because what matters most is that you incorporate the vibration of the oil into your magic.

Many people say that synthetic oils do not work as well as pure essential oils; that the magic is not as powerful when the oils are not all-natural. We do not agree with this, and that opinion is based on our own experience. Way before HOI, back when we knew nothing about oils, we only used the materials we had on hand. Many of them were synthetic and that never prevented us from generating the results we desired from our rituals. Today, we do tend to use more organic and natural products because we have more access and resources. The bottom line is that you should never let your rituals or magical practice suffer simply because you don't believe you have the "right" tools at your disposal.

EXTRA MAGICAL SUPPORT

WITH THESE BASIC TOOLS AT YOUR DISPOSAL, YOU CAN ALSO INCORPORATE additional elements to enhance and activate your magic as you wish and as your intuition guides you to. We will offer suggestions for some of these extras in the rituals included in the book, but you should always default to what feels right to you.

TIMING

THE TRUTH OF THE MATTER IS THAT YOU CAN—AND SHOULD!—PERFORM RITUALS and magic whenever you feel moved to do so and require some cosmic support, guidance, or protection. However, if you are working with magic that doesn't feel so time sensitive, you can consider what timing might be most supportive of your intention.

ASTROLOGICAL CYCLES

WE TIME A LOT OF OUR RITUALS AROUND THE CYCLES OF THE MOON. IN OUR MIND, there is a lot to be said for working with the natural rhythms and cycles of Mother Nature. These cycles act as a super boost of energy, and that is especially the case with the nurturing feminine spirit of the moon.

Every month includes at least one new moon and full moon. The new moon represents the beginning of cycles, so it's a great time to perform rituals that have to do with ushering things into your life, whether it's a new job, more money, a relationship, or a different type of energy than what you are currently experiencing. Full moons, on the other hand, are a time of release and completion. This is the time for letting things go, whether it's a chapter of your life, a person, or an emotion that's holding you down.

The options for both of these cycles are more or less endless, because so much of life is about the constant nature of bringing in new and releasing old as we adapt, change, and evolve, constantly moving along the path that is our highest good.

As you perform these lunar rituals, you will want to take note of which zodiac sign the new or full moon is occurring in and use the energy of that sign to amplify your ritual. For example, when the moon is in sexy, mysterious Scorpio, you can be sure that Marlene is mixing up a love spell to get Alex's attention. (For more on new and full moon rituals, see pages 241 and 244.)

Another cosmic cycle that we like to take into consideration is Mercury Retrograde. Even if you're not into astrology, chances are you've spent enough time on Instagram to see memes that give you an idea of what Mercury Retrograde is about. Technically, Mercury Retrograde is when Mercury (the planet that governs communications) appears to be moving backward from the vantage point of Earth. It is known to be a time during which situations can go awry, communication breakdowns occur, things break down (particularly electronic devices), and when people or situations from our past may stage a reappearance.

We like to time rituals that involve clear communication with Mercury Retrograde. One of our favorites to use during this period is Candle Magic for Peace and Harmony (see page 192), because it involves the throat chakra and can counteract communication that is murky or unclear.

DAYS OF THE WEEK

IN ADDITION TO THE HEAVENLY CYCLES, THERE IS ALSO AN ENERGY TO EACH DAY OF the week. As is the case with astrological timing, you should always perform rituals when you feel called to do so. But for extra potency and activation, consider timing your ritual so that it aligns with the day of the week that best matches the energy of your intention.

- **MONDAY—dreams, road opening, spiritual growth**
- **TUESDAY—removing obstacles, strength, victory**
- **WEDNESDAY—ancestors, self-love**
- **THURSDAY—legal matters, money**
- **FRIDAY—fertility, love**
- **SATURDAY—banishing, creativity, motivation**
- **SUNDAY—healing, health, peace**

NUMEROLOGY

IF YOU PRACTICE NUMEROLOGY, YOU ALREADY KNOW THAT NUMBERS CAN BE POWerful, and it's probably not surprising that they are yet another element that can be weaved into magic. We have learned this time and time again in our own practice. Numbers are a subtle way of specifying magic and allowing intuition to guide you as you go. We use numbers to correspond to angels, deities, and significant personal meanings that apply to both ourselves and our ancestors.

Numbers can be brought into ritual in a lot of different ways. For example, you might perform a ritual at a certain time of day or night based on the symbolism associated with the number of an hour. Or you might add a specific number of drops of oil to a ritual based on what you want to invoke. You might recite a mantra a specific number of times. With this in mind, if you see, for instance, that one of the rituals included in this book calls for three herbs, but you feel called to include five instead, by all means, follow that guidance.

These are a few of our go-to number symbols but, remember the numbers that work for you may very well be quite personal and differ from these. As always, let your intuition guide you.

- **3—completion of work**
- **5—abundance, love, money**
- **7—fertility, growth**
- **21—road opening**

COLORS

COLORS ARE A GREAT ELEMENT TO INCORPORATE INTO MAGICAL RITUALS AND TO use as a means of carrying rituals and intentions into your daily life. Because of their vibrational energy, colors help establish mood, both for ourselves and the people who we are interacting with, which can serve to ignite our intentions. Colors are also a helpful and powerful tool for working through emotion and healing.

Even if you've never heard of this power colors have before, you've probably felt it when you wear a certain color or are in a room where the walls seem to cast a certain vibe or energy. Colors can evoke emotion, and emotion is energy—a very powerful form of energy.

The next time you are in ritual, or even getting dressed for a meeting or a big date, think about the energy you want to bring into the room. As you select the elements for your ritual, such as candles or pieces of cloth, think about which colors are symbolic of what you want to accomplish.

Following is a guide to color symbolism; however, as always, follow your intuition where it leads you.

- **BLACK—removal of negative energy and obstacles, reversal work, uncrossing**
- **DARK BLUE—communication, healing, peace**
- **BROWN—balance, meditation, nurturing**
- **GREEN—creativity, energizing, financial and business success, good luck, inspiration, removal of money obstacles**

- **LAVENDER—divination, inner healing, marriage, peace**
- **ORANGE—career success, creativity, energizing, goals, inspiration, sex**
- **LIGHT PINK—companionship, friendship, spiritual development**
- **DARK PURPLE—connecting with your intuition, dreamwork, psychic development**
- **RED—love, passion, sex**
- **WHITE—removal of negative energy, reversal work, uncrossing**
- **YELLOW—abundance, creativity, wisdom**

SPIRITUAL ASSISTANCE

BY NOW YOU'VE PROBABLY NOTICED THAT WE FREQUENTLY REFER TO AND CALL upon ancestors, angels, and spirit. These entities are available to all of us, although you may call them something different than we do. There exists a team of invisible forces that are invested in our highest good and here to help activate our own power and magic, if only we call upon them. Yes, you are powerful in and of yourself, but that power is multiplied when you have entities from the Other Side pulling on your behalf.

Over the years, the two of us have developed a very real relationship with our ancestors, angels, and spirit. We talk to them, we pray to them, we make offerings to them on our altar. Not only do we feel that this enhances the power of our ritual and intentions, but it also serves as a constant reminder that we are connected to something much bigger than ourselves. This can happen in so many different ways—it might be through electricity, doors opening or closing, meaningful objects appearing or disappearing, a waft of perfume, or a meaningful song playing on the radio at just the right moment. However spirit shows up for you, the most important thing is to acknowledge it when it happens.

They are here for you, if only you ask. In addition to requesting their help when necessary, also be sure to express love and gratitude on a regular basis.

PART THREE

RITUALS

CHAPTER FIVE

BUILDING YOUR SPIRITUAL ARSENAL

RITUALS AND MAGIC ARE CLOSELY RELATED, BUT THEY ARE NOT THE SAME. RITUALS can be a way of life, a practice that keeps us connected and on our path. For example, a masseuse might perform the ritual of scrubbing their hands on a regular basis for the purpose of keeping their energy clear. It's a habit, a way of life. Or, take Alex, for instance: She regularly carries a stone that represents communication with her into meetings. Ritual might also look like using salt in the bathtub or jumping in the ocean to keep your aura clean and maintain the highest vibration possible. Think of rituals as preventive care that paves the way for magic to more easily enter your life. Magic comes in when there is a need. We can use rituals to access that magic in an intentional way.

Rituals don't have to be complex or showy, and they can fit easily into busy, modern day-to-day life. You don't have to do extreme things like tripping on ayahuasca in the jungle (we've tried it—didn't like it). You don't have to pay hundreds or even thousands of dollars for "professional" guidance or for a retreat to a mystical place. We can't say it enough: You don't need a guru, elder, or advanced practitioner to guide you through rituals. Including us. All we are here to do is offer suggestions to get you started. If, at any point, we offer a suggestion that doesn't resonate with you, then, by all means, follow your own instincts.

Most important in all of this is that your rituals come from you and that you acknowledge and follow your own guidance in the process of performing those rituals. Rituals can look any which way and involve all kinds of different facets of life. If you want to create a ritual about something, you can. And you get to design that ritual in whatever way calls to you.

PUT YOUR INTUITION INTO PRACTICE

IN THE PAGES TO COME, YOU WILL FIND A VARIETY OF RITUALS FOR RELATIONSHIPS, success, protection, healing, and cleansing. Allow your intuition to lead you to the one you need the most at any given moment in time. Don't go on a magical bonanza and do them all at once. That's the equivalent of sending fifty smoke signals out at once—the universe won't know where to send its attention and energy. We see this happen all the time when, for example, a client comes into the store and purchases love, creativity, and money candles at the same time. As you practice, be specific about your intentions and desires. Allow yourself to *really* go through the process and to listen to the response the universe sends in answer to your request. We all have many desires, but you can't get all of them at the same time any more than you can effectively pursue a multitude of career paths simultaneously.

We have included two types of rituals in this book. First are our Tried and True practices. These are the rituals that the two of us have used time and time again over the years and that we suggest to our clients the most frequently when they come to us with various desires, situations, and ailments. We will provide these tried and true ritual practices from beginning to end. Of course, you can always tweak them if you feel called to, but we are offering the rituals in the same way that we practice them ourselves.

The second type of ritual are what we call the intuition-led rituals. For these, we have provided a short list of base ingredients to act as the foundation of your ritual. Following that, you will find a selection of various herbs and oils and crystals that you can choose among or, alternatively, you can use all of them. Think of it as a choose-your-own-adventure practice. Making these selections will require you to tap into your intuition to notice which ingredients call out to you. As you go through the list of options, notice what calls to you, even as a gentle tug or whisper, and go with those. Of course, you can also always use ingredients that aren't included on the list at all. Follow your intuition and see where it leads you. Discover how much information you innately know—or, more accurately, are innately able to call in.

The rituals provided in this book—and especially the intuition-led rituals—are meant to act as inspiration and suggestions, rather than directions. It's for this reason that you often won't find specific measurements or quantities for ingredients. These rituals aren't designed to be specific like recipes you might find in a cookbook. We want you to find your way through and to listen to yourself in the process (while, of course, also being mindful of Mother Nature's resources). It's important to us that, in this process, you have the opportunity to access your intuition, learn to trust yourself, and make your own magic. We want you to see verification of the magic that exists around you on a regular and ongoing basis and the knowledge that you already hold within. That's why we've built the practice of putting your own intuition to work into the intuition-led rituals included in this book.

Over the years, we have done enough rituals that we have come to understand what many different ingredients symbolize. But, still, most of our magic comes from intuition. Every time we prepare and are in ritual, we make a point of being as intuitively open as possible. We can't even tell you how many times an ingredient has popped into our minds to be included in a spell, only for us to understand later that its symbolic meaning is uncannily linked to what we were trying to bring in. So, follow your own lead. If you read through a ritual and have an inkling that something should be added or swapped in, do that. And then, after the fact, find out what the symbolism of that ingredient is, because it will help you build trust in your own intuition once you have your own uncanny experiences.

With all of this in mind, we have included an appendix at the end of this book (see page 248) that explains what each of the ingredients included in the rituals symbolizes. However, we ask that you not cross-reference the appendix until *after* you've finished your ritual. Rather than leaning on the appendix for guidance, use it as a system of checks and balances to build up your confidence in yourself and your intuition. We're willing to bet that you'll be shocked when you flip to the back of the book and realize how specific the choices you've made are to your situation. Do this enough times, and you will stop questioning your intuition altogether.

BEING IN THE STATE OF RITUAL

RITUALS ARE NOT A MOMENT IN TIME; THEY ARE A PROCESS AND A STATE OF BEING. From this state of being, you stir up and infuse everything around you—and yourself—with the energy you are trying to create. You are powering up both yourself and the world around you. You are activating.

Rituals begin long before you sit down to perform the active part of the ritual. They start at the moment you start to prepare. This means that when you get in the car and drive to the market to buy some herbs or walk out to the garden to select some flowers, you are in ritual. As you choose your ingredients, be intentional about remaining in a state of gratitude to Mother Earth and all of your helpers for providing and guiding you toward what you need. When you pick a rosemary sprig from your garden or at Whole Foods, thank Mother Earth for the resources she has provided. When you combine your ingredients together, you are in ritual. After you have actively performed your ritual, you remain in ritual. You are aware of your intention. You are in communication with the entities you're working in tandem with—your spirit guides and ancestors, the angels, source.

We would all be better off if we lived our entire lives in a state of ritual but, of course, we are humans, so that's not really possible. With that in mind, just as important as creating an intentional and sustained state of ritual is closing it out when the time is right. This is done with one final expression of gratitude to Mother Earth, which can be as simple as "thank you."

RITUAL BASICS

THERE ARE A FEW BASICS THAT APPLY TO EVERY RITUAL YOU PERFORM. YOU CAN think of them as your magical best practices.

INTENTION

Each ritual will include an intention. That intention might be something you want to manifest, or it might be a more general state of gratitude. This intention will be your point of focus the entire way through the ritual, from preparation to disposal. If you have a ritual that extends over a period of time, such as candle magic, you will come back to that intention every time you begin again.

ENVIRONMENT

You prepare for and invite your spirit friends into your home in much the same way you would your human friends. Begin by tidying up your space; only in this case you'll do that by cleansing and clearing with incense, herbs, or resins. Then, call upon your intended guests. Go to the altar and let your ancestors, source, angels, and whatever other light beings resonate with you know that you would like them to join you.

TOOLS

When you are using a bowl to combine ingredients, always use glass, not plastic. Glass is of the earth; plastic is manmade. Also, use tools that are specifically reserved for your magical practice. If you are using a bowl to combine your ritual ingredients, don't use the same bowl for your Cheerios the next morning. Use one that is reserved specifically for the purposes of magic. These tools should be considered sacred.

That doesn't mean they have to be expensive or otherwise specialized, just that they are exclusively for spiritual rather than material usage.

INFUSION

As you add your ingredients to your ritual, infuse yourself into each and every one of them. What does that mean? Well, if you're using herbs, for instance, put your hands on them, touch them, merge your energy with theirs. As you do this, not only will you infuse your ingredients, but you also simultaneously cleanse them. Cleansing is done by pulling white light from the heavens down through your crown (located at the top of your head). To do this, simply visualize white light streaming down from the heavens, through your crown, down through your throat, into your chest, then down your arms, through your fingertips, and into the ingredients.

ALTAR

Your altar will play a role in almost all of your rituals, even if the active part of your ritual does not occur at the altar. For example, you will take your ritual bath in the bathroom, but still light a candle on your altar. It is through your altar that you call the attention of your spirits and ancestors to ask for their assistance with your intention. If you don't already have one, we will walk you through setting up an altar at the end of this chapter.

OFFERINGS

With that in mind, you will notice that several of the rituals in this book include offerings. Again, whether you are performing the ritual at your altar or not, you will want to place this offering on your altar for your ancestors to express gratitude for their assistance. In many of the intuition-led rituals, we have included a variety of offering options that align with the energy of the ritual. However, you know what your ancestors liked best during their time on this earth, so feel free to personalize your offering to their preferences as a remembrance.

DISPOSAL

Going back to the idea that rituals last beyond the duration of the physical act of ritual, it's important to be intentional about how you dispose of the ingredients used in your ritual once you have completed it. Where applicable, we will offer suggestions for how you might release your ritual ingredients in a way that is aligned with your intention.

This idea of disposal applies to anything that has been blessed on your altar and is, thus, sacred. That means that extra herbs that have not been included on your candle for anointing purposes or incorporated in your bath mixture, for example, do not need to be disposed of in an intentional way since they have not been blessed. A candle that has been burned down on your altar, on the other hand, should be disposed of in an intentional way that aligns with the energy of the ritual.

EVERY RITUAL MATTERS

ONE LAST NOTE BEFORE YOU DIVE IN: IT'S IMPORTANT TO UNDERSTAND THAT THERE is no such thing as an unsuccessful ritual. Sometimes the intentions behind your rituals will manifest—this will likely become the case more and more frequently as you build your faith and tap into your intuition to better understand yourself, your life path, and your highest good. Other times, though, your intention will not be brought into being.

When the intention behind a ritual does not come to fruition, know that there is just as much reason and purpose for that as there is for when it does. Whether an intention manifests or not, every single ritual you perform strengthens your relationship with spirit, which ultimately benefits you in every way and on every level. And *that* is the real magic behind rituals. You can trust that your highest good is always being guarded.

As time goes on and you do more rituals, they will become like second nature to you. Chances are, you will consult this book less and less, and listen to your inner voice more and more. You may even find that you begin to live your life as a series of rituals without even thinking about it. Like other forms of habitual wellness, rituals evolve over time from a practice to a lifestyle.

START HERE: CREATE YOUR ALTAR

ONE FINAL, IMPORTANT STEP BEFORE WE MOVE INTO OUR RITUAL PRACTICE, IS TO create your altar. This will serve as the touchstone of your magical practice. Even if you never do a single other ritual, just the act of creating and using an altar will bring you much closer to magic, intuition, spirit, and your ancestors.

Your altar will serve as your sacred little corner in your home. It's where you will go to meditate, pray, communicate, and connect with your ancestors, guides, and the universe. Your altar doesn't have to be elaborate or big, it just has to be yours, and reserved for this one specific and important purpose. Setting up an altar doesn't require a lot of time, expense, or even space. It just involves tuning in to what feels meaningful to you. That will look different for everyone.

It's completely possible to have an altar in plain sight that visitors don't even recognize as such. (Although we don't necessarily recommend this, simply because you will want your altar in a safe, peaceful space, which often means a space with less traffic.) The first important thing to understand about your altar is that it should, above all else, be specific to you. Your altar will pay tribute to the people and objects that are most sacred and meaningful to you and that remind you of who you are, who you are supported by, and where you want to go in life. The only thing we recommend you *don't* include on your altar is pictures of the living because you want to keep them associated with the material world for as long as possible. Other than that, let your imagination fly free!

As a testament to this idea of individuality, each of our altars looks very different. Marlene's includes a cross from her aunt's funeral, as well as a picture of her aunt and grandmother. Many of the contents on her altar change on a regular basis, depending upon what Marlene is working on at any given moment. For example, if Marlene is working on a project on the altar, she'll include a piece of paper with the names of the people she's working on it with and deadlines. It helps her to remain focused and stay in gratitude for her life in the present moment.

Since hummingbirds have always been a totem for Alex dating back to her childhood, her altar includes a little hummingbird she found and lovingly placed in a wooden coffin. It serves as a constant reminder to Alex that she is guarded and protected by hummingbirds. She also keeps a rosary, her grandmother's picture, and a statue of Saint Anthony that her grandmother gave to her when she was young there.

PLACEMENT

Begin by choosing a table, shelf, or platform to set up your altar on. Select a place that feels inviting, comfortable, safe, quiet, and perhaps even sacred to you. You can do this anywhere in your home, with the exception of your bedroom.

Once you've found your location, clear the area of any dust, debris, or clutter to prep it. Then open the windows nearby the place where you plan to set up your altar and burn your favorite incense, resin, or sage to energetically cleanse and clear the space. Finally, add the altar pieces (guidance on selecting them follows) in the order that resonates most with you.

KEEP IT OUTTA THE BEDROOM

Bedrooms are reserved for physical acts (you know what we're talking about!), and your altar is designed to connect you with *unearthly* elements, so it's best to keep these two energies separate.

If, by chance, your bedroom is your only option for altar placement, be sure not to perform any acts in front of your altar that you wouldn't want your parents to see. If need be, you can make your altar small enough to take down when necessary, place it in your closet, or cover it as a form of respect.

THE FOUR ELEMENTS

You will want the four elements of Earth represented on your altar: fire, air, water, and earth. These are the elements that sustain us, and this representation is a way of paying homage and expressing gratitude.

Water is an important element of your altar because it holds cleansing properties. Choose a chalice, goblet, or glass to hold the water in. Once this glass is placed on your altar, it becomes a sacred object—this means that, like any other tool you use in your rituals, it's not to be used for everyday purposes from that point forward. As you pray over your altar, the water will continue to become more and more blessed. Over time, you can use the water from this glass in lieu of holy water from a temple or church for your gratitude rituals or blessings. Note that you will not want to use your holy water for rituals that have to do with banishing or negativity.

In addition to water, the water element can also be represented by beverages such as coffee, wine, or any other drink that your ancestors enjoyed. Just be sure not to leave these beverages out indefinitely, for the very practical reason that you will ultimately end up with a mostly evaporated, syrupy sludge at the bottom of your glass. Just like you wouldn't want to serve this to dinner guests, you don't want to serve it to your spiritual guests, either.

Incense is a powerful addition to an altar, because it represents not just one element, but two: earth and air. Resin can be used to represent these two elements as well.

Crystals can be used to represent the earth element, as can herbs and flowers.

Candles can be used to represent the fire and air elements.

You might also use a feather, bell, or wind chimes to represent air.

These are the most commonly found objects on altars of all types; however, more important than using these specific items is making sure that each of the four elements is accounted for on your altar.

THE PERSONAL TOUCH

In addition to including objects to draw in the four elements, you can include items that are personally meaningful to you or that make you feel connected to something greater than yourself. This might include things like pictures of your ancestors or any heirlooms or tokens that remind you of and connect you to them.

If you feel magnetized to a spirit animal—which we believe everyone is—you can also include a representation of it on your altar. Animal totems are designed to guide us through life. If there is an animal that you see frequently or at uncanny times, or if you feel connected to a specific animal for reasons you can't quite explain, chances are that's your totem. This animal can be represented on your altar in any number of ways. Let's say you feel connected to eagles: You might include a picture of an eagle, a figurine of an eagle, or a feather.

In addition to being the place where you pray, meditate, and express gratitude, your altar is also a place where you can set your intentions and keep your rituals once they are complete if you so choose. To include intentions on your altar, all you have to do is write them out and place them among your sacred objects. You can also use your altar to infuse objects with your intentions. For example, we sometimes place contracts on our altar to infuse them with our energy and intentions—after all, this *is* modern magic, and it's designed to enhance our daily lives!

CHAPTER SIX

TRIED AND TRUE RITUALS

IN THIS CHAPTER YOU WILL FIND THE RITUALS THAT WE GO BACK TO TIME AND TIME again, many of which predate HOI. Some of these rituals are inspired by classic spells or magic that others have shared with us over the years. Others are rituals that we created with our own intuition.

Because we use these rituals so often, we tend to follow them the way they are presented on the pages to come. However, if you feel called to tweak or swap out ingredients, you should certainly feel free to do so.

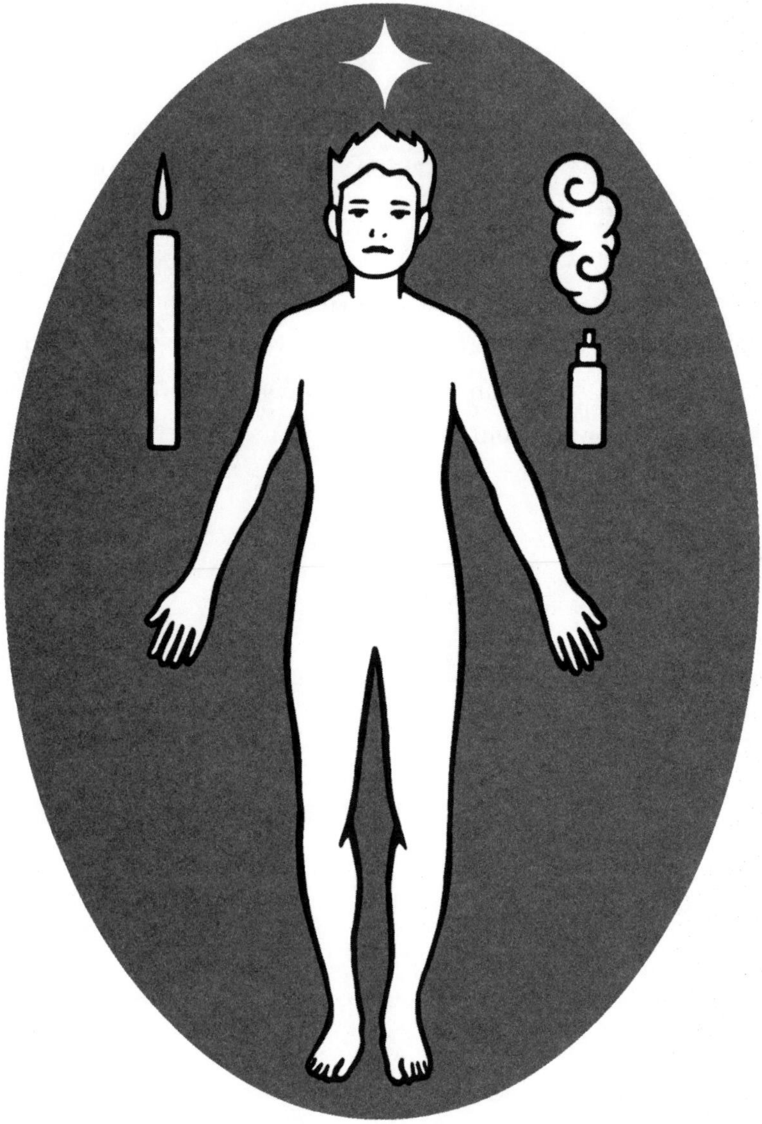

AURA CLEANSING SPRAY

From a young age, we're taught about hygiene for our physical body, but no one really talks about energetic hygiene, which is just as important.

This Aura Cleansing Spray is like taking your aura through a car wash. Just like you want to keep your car looking clean and shiny, you want to maintain your aura's natural vibrancy.

As a human, you are a magnetic being. While you walk through your day minding your own business, your body is constantly drawing things to it in much the same way dust naturally builds up in your home. Just like removing dust leaves your house feeling lighter and brighter, this spray will lift energetic stagnation and make you feel clearer and more buoyant.

This spray should be used on a regular basis, and especially during those times when you feel heavy or stuck. Just spritz it on yourself like you would with perfume. As you spritz it over yourself, recite the mantra: *Remove and cleanse my aura of all that does not serve me. Renew and make room for what serves my highest good with every drop that touches my being.*

As you'll see, this ritual calls for an amber bottle to store the spray in. This is important for storage in any ritual that utilizes oils, because the amber keeps the oil from going rancid over time. You can find these easily at local craft stores.

INGREDIENTS

- Pinch of Epsom salt
- Distilled water to fill your spray container
- Camphor
- Lavender
- Sage

SUPPLIES

- Amber spray bottle

Put the Epsom salt into your spray container, then fill the bottle almost to the top with distilled water. Add the camphor, lavender, and sage to your preference, using your sense of smell to guide you. Twist the top on your bottle and gently shake it to incorporate the ingredients. Place the spray bottle on your altar and set your intention.

After your spray bottle has sat on your altar for at least 24 hours, remove and use as desired. Sprays should generally be kept in a cooler environment out of direct sunlight, but the truth is that we tend to carry a bottle of Aura Cleansing Spray with us wherever we go.

PURIFICATION SPRAY

We first made this spray in 2010, and more than a decade later we *still* have a big mason jar full of that first batch. We suggest using this mixture sparingly because it requires a lot of ingredients. Luckily, the addition of vodka keeps everything fresh, so just continue to add water to the jar over time to keep it going strong.

We tend to use this spray in much the same way people use Raid to get rid of a bug. If an energy that we don't like or that makes us uneasy enters our space, we spray the area they walked through once they leave to purify any lingering energy.

INGREDIENTS

- 3 bay leaves
- 5 cinnamon sticks
- 10 star anise
- 1 cup jasmine flower petals
- 2 cups rosebuds
- 1 cup orange peels
- ⅓ cup vodka
- 3 cups distilled water
- 7 drops eucalyptus essential oil
- 7 drops lavender essential oil
- 7 drops sage essential oil

SUPPLIES

- Glass bowl, for ritual use
- Tealight candle
- Airtight jar, such as a mason jar
- Amber spray bottle

Place the bay leaves, cinnamon sticks, star anise, jasmine flower petals, rosebuds, orange peels, and vodka in a large pot. Place the pot over a low flame, cover it, and allow it to simmer for a minimum of 3 hours.

Strain the mixture. You can use the strained ingredients for another purpose (such as a ritual bath) or dispose of them since they have not yet been blessed on your altar. Allow the liquid to cool, then place the mixture in a glass bowl on your altar.

Light the tealight candle, set an intention, and allow the bowl to remain on your altar for a minimum of 24 hours.

When you are ready, remove the bowl from your altar and add the distilled water, eucalyptus, lavender, and sage oils, and stir.

Place the mixture in an airtight jar. Transfer the mixture to an amber spray bottle to use it as a spray or, alternatively, add 4 ounces of the mixture to a bucket of water to use it as a floor wash.

DOUBLE DUTY

Most sprays can do double duty as a floor wash by adding 4 ounces of the base mixture of the spray to a bucket filled with water.

Floor washes are Alex's jam. They will serve the dual purposes of physically cleaning your floors thanks to the vodka, and—*bonus!*—spiritually creating an energetic sense of grounding and stability. It's important to bring this type of energy in because floors serve as the foundation of your home, both literally and figuratively.

Before using the floor wash, sweep your floor as you normally would to remove dirt, dust, and debris. Then, use either a mop or a cloth and elbow grease to cleanse the surface of your floor with the wash. Allow the wash to dry.

ANCHOR YOUR HOME

While other spells in this book cleanse and purify the inside of your home (such as Coconut House Cleanse on page 150), this ritual provides a spiritual shield or bright energetic field around the entire property your house is situated on. It secures the energetic foundation upon which you build your life and your family.

We work with a graphic designer named Jaakko. When he first came to us, Jaakko wasn't exactly into candles, crystals, and magic. He was into partying and the music scene. But Jaakko was great at what he did, we loved his aesthetic, and we loved him.

One night, Jaakko called us. We could hear in his voice that he was frantic. A local wildfire was bearing down on his house to the point where he could see it coming from his backyard. He'd done all of the logistical things you're supposed to do in that situation; he watered his roof and soaked his yard but, intuitively, he knew that wasn't enough. He needed a fast answer from us about what he could do to energetically protect his home from disaster. Over the phone, as Jaakko was understandably freaking out, we walked him through the process of anchoring down the four corners of his house and property, praying and asking Mother Earth and the heavens for protection as he went. Just hearing his voice in that moment was terrifying.

What do you know? At the last minute, the winds picked up and took the fire in the opposite direction of his home. All around Jaakko, homes had been tragically burned to the ground. Meanwhile, his remained standing, untouched.

We're so grateful that Jaakko's story has a happy ending. And, in a pinch, this ritual can be performed in a moment of need, as Jaakko did. (It's also worth noting that, since Jaakko was in dire straits, his version of this ritual looked a bit different from the version included in this book.) But you might be able to spare yourself some drama later on down the line by securing your property anytime you purchase a new house. You can also perform it for your friends' and loved ones' homes—with their permission, of course.

The railroad nails included in this ritual—which you can often find lying around railroad tracks or, more simply, order from Amazon—pay tribute to Ogun. Ogun is a deity associated with railroad tracks, and is known for being both a warrior and a protector.

The earth that your home sits on has a history and an energy. This spell blesses and purifies that earth, and will control the type of energy that treads on that land for the duration of your time on the property. While we suggest people do this ritual upon moving into a new home, if you haven't yet anchored your home, you can do it at any point to create a strong foundation for your personal place of protection and shelter.

INGREDIENTS

4 large railroad nails

Handful of coffee beans

36 pennies

Palm oil (corojo)

Handful of dried corn kernels

Tobacco, taken from a cigar

SUPPLIES

White plate, for ritual use

Brown candle

Hammer

Use water from the faucet of your home to clean the railroad nails, and allow them to dry.

Once the nails are dry, rub palm oil over them as you focus on anchoring your new home and creating a strong foundation for yourself and your family.

Place the white plate on your altar and add the coffee beans, corn kernels, pennies, and tobacco. Place the railroad nails on top of the other ingredients. Light the brown candle on your altar and set your intention for your new home.

When the candle has burned all the way down, take your plate (with the contents still on it) and a hammer outside. Starting on the back-left side of your property and moving from there to the right-back, then to the left-front and right-front side of your property, hammer 1 nail into each corner. Place 9 pennies around each nail and sprinkle the mixture from the plate on top of them to seal the spell. As you do this, visualize your home secure and locked into Mother Earth. Claim and secure your property to protect it from being taken from you.

MATTRESS BLESSING

We tend to think of mattresses as utilitarian, but they are also very symbolic—mattresses represent and hold our dreams, our home, and our body. Not only that, but think about what a large percentage of your life you spend on your mattress! And, yet, have you ever once stopped to think about the energy of it? Most people haven't.

Mattresses are an important element of our homes to bless because as we lie on them we are in our most vulnerable state. It's also the state in which we are visited by spirit and in which we can go to other spiritual realms.

There's a very human element to the Mattress Blessing, as well. It will also keep you and your partner connected in the same energy field even as you sleep. And, if you're single, this blessing is still powerful because it offers a buffet of goodness, including blessings of abundance, love, physical and emotional health, and spiritual support.

This is one of those rituals we think everyone should do. You only have to do it once in the lifetime of your mattress, unless you split from the person you share your mattress with or otherwise intuitively feel like something needs to shift.

INGREDIENTS

1 bill of any denomination

1 rose petal, the color of your choice

1 eucalyptus leaf

1 orange peel

Moonstone crystal

Gold candle

Peppermint oil

SUPPLIES

White bowl, for ritual use

Place the bill, rose petal, eucalyptus leaf, orange peel, and moonstone crystal in the white bowl and put it on your altar along with the gold candle. Light your candle and set your intention for this blessing. As the candle burns, anoint your bill with the peppermint oil as you set an intention for abundance.

Once the candle has burned down, take the bowl with your ingredients into your bedroom or wherever the mattress you want to bless is. Remove the mattress from your box spring or bed stand and place your ingredients on the box spring or bed stand as follows, reciting an intention as you place each ingredient:

- **Top left corner of the bed (money corner)—bill**
- **Top right corner of the bed (love corner)—rose petal**
- **Bottom left corner of the bed (health)—eucalyptus leaf**
- **Bottom right corner of the bed (happiness, inspiration, and creativity)—orange peel**
- **Center of the bed (connection to spirit, the universe, and your higher self)—moonstone crystal**

Replace your mattress, leaving your offerings underneath it. To amplify and continually activate this blessing, you may repeat your intentions as desired each time you lie in your bed.

COCONUT HOUSE CLEANSE

This spell is wonderfully witchy. It's one of our all-time favorite rituals, and one that we use a lot. Not only does the Coconut House Cleanse remove unwanted energies, but it also invites in your spirits, ancestors, and angels. One thing you should know before you start this ritual is that this takes more energy than you might think, especially if you live in a large home.

Coconuts pack in a lot of very powerful energy because not only do they represent purity, but they're also known as an offering for the gods. As you'll see, the coconut is kicked throughout your home, but never picked up while you are inside of your home. This is because the coconut is being used to pull any unwanted energy out of your space, so you don't want to pick up and handle the energy within your home.

This spell offers the option of Florida Water in place of holy water. Florida Water is a common perfume that was first created in the 1800s and used in Victorian times. It's named Florida Water as a reference to the Fountain of Youth, which is said to be located in Florida (maybe that explains why so many people retire there!). Florida Water has long been recognized as plant medicine in the spiritual world and considered effective for lifting negative energy. Witches frequently used Florida Water to remove entities and possessions, but it's also a very mainstream product that can be found at CVS.

Do a Coconut House Cleanse when you first move into a home, much like you would do a physical deep clean. You should also use it anytime you sense an uninvited presence or energy in your home, or if you have a child who mentions seeing something in the house.

Remember, children tend to be more tuned in than adults, so there's every chance your child is picking up on something you are unaware of. This cleanse is also good for businesses that involve the kind of work that results in a lot of emotional or energetic residue.

INGREDIENTS

Holy water or Florida Water	**Coconut, with all hairs removed**	**Crushed eggshell (cascarilla)**

Sprinkle your water onto the coconut and let it dry. Once the coconut is dry, rub the cascarilla all over it, until the coconut is completely white.

Take your coconut to the back of the space you want to cleanse (the point furthest from the front door). If you have a multistory home, start on the highest floor and move your way down. While praying, reciting a prayer or affirmation, or visualizing, place the coconut on the floor and kick it from one corner to the next until you have covered the entire perimeter of the room. Remaining focused on your intention the entire time, continue moving through the house like this until you reach the front door.

When you reach the front door, push the coconut outside with your foot, then pick it up and walk it out to the street. As you stand at the edge of the curb, inhale deeply through your nose, filling your belly with air, and visualize gathering all of the emotions of fear and negativity from your space and being. Hold the air in your belly until it feels right to release it. When you're ready to exhale, lift the coconut up to the height of your mouth and about 6 inches in front of it. As if you were fogging up a mirror, exhale all the air out of your belly and onto the coconut. In doing this, you are infusing the coconut with the power of your essence and the life force of your breath.

Lift the coconut above your head and express gratitude to your God, higher self, ancestors, guides, and whoever else feels appropriate to you. Then throw the coconut down onto the pavement as hard as you can. As the coconut shatters and splinters, it is breaking up all of the negativity both within your space and within you.

Pick up the pieces of the coconut and toss them in a trash can that is not located on your property. You might consider depositing them at a trash can in a church as an offering.

TRADER JOE'S DOESN'T CARRY HOLY WATER—WHAT DO I DO?!

Holy water can be found at any church or temple. Just bring a container to your religious institution of choice, and they will happily fill it up with holy water for your use. Trust us, they get this request more than you would guess!

Alternatively, as you pray over your altar, any water you place on it will continue to become more and more blessed. Over time, you can use the water from that glass in lieu of holy water from a temple or church for your rituals.

OUT, DAMN SPIRITS!

Okay, we know that, especially if you're new to magic, you're probably thinking this spell is not for you. You don't have spirits in *your* home, and just the thought of it is a little bit creepy.

The truth of the matter is that energy is for real and, because of that, this is one of those spells that we believe should be done in every home. Every person who has ever walked this earth—including Mother Teresa—has a light side and a dark side. That darkness has nothing to do with being evil, it has to do with being human. The same is true of the spirit world. Sometimes bright lights come in and attach themselves to our beings; other times dark ones do. Like humans, these spirits are not evil, they are simply of a lower vibration that doesn't serve us.

You have no idea what the people who come into your home are bringing through the door with them, nor do you know what may have happened in your house before you arrived. Unfortunately, you can't exactly check the aura of each visitor before they come through the door, nor can you get a write-up about the energetic past of your house from the realtor, so this spell is the next best thing. It offers your home protection, no matter what kind of energy comes through the door.

Now, having said that: Remember that the purpose of this ritual is specifically to get rid of *unwanted* energy in your home or energy that doesn't belong to you.

Case in point: People used to consider the two of us somewhat of an energetic housecleaning service. One day, a woman called us in to clear spirits from her home. As we did so, Marlene paused by the couch.

"Are you sure you want us to get rid of *everything*?" she asked the owner.

The owner quickly nodded in reply.

"Did you recently lose a sister?" Marlene pressed.

"Yes," the woman gasped.

It turned out this woman didn't want to get rid of *everything* in her house, after all.

Many of us have kind, helpful energies that follow us around from place to place. So, when you're doing an energetic cleanse such as this one, it's important to be specific. Tap into your intuition and feel into the presences around you. Feel into their energy and intention, and make known which ones you want to let go of, and which ones you want to keep right there with you.

INGREDIENTS

Black tourmaline crystal
Camphor block or oil
1 garlic clove
1 cup sea salt
1 teaspoon vinegar
1 cup water
Black candle

SUPPLIES

Bowl, for ritual use

Place the black tourmaline crystal, camphor block, garlic clove, salt, vinegar, and water into a bowl, then place your bowl on the altar.

Light the black candle on your altar and set your intention for protection. Allow the candle to burn all of the way down and, only then, remove the bowl from your altar.

Place the bowl with the mixture in it under your bed or on the floor next to your bed while you sleep to keep any unwanted spirits from disrupting you. You can also place the bowl on the floor behind your front door to keep spirits from entering your home with visitors.

CUT IT OUT

Cord-cutting is a spiritual practice in which you release the power that people, behaviors, or situations have over your energy. This spell is a way of energetically cutting those energies and influences off so that you are no longer affected by them.

Most people perform this spell to cut the cord from a person who was formerly in their life. Even when someone is no longer actively in your life, you can still be energetically attached to them. You've probably experienced this before. Say, for instance, you break up with someone, but continue to think about them all the time. Or you ended a friendship several months or even years ago, and yet you continue to feel agitated by that person. This spell works well for relationships of any variety that have hit a dead end and require a clean break. Before performing this spell, make sure that you are really ready to release that person once and for all.

When you perform this spell, not only do you release yourself from the other person's energy, but you also release that person from any energetic hold you might have over them as well. This spell has nothing to do with malice; it's about letting two people move along their separate paths without obsessing about each other's Instagram pages.

But, again, it's not just for cutting the energetic cords other people have in your life. The two of us perform this ritual on a regular basis, and it's usually because we want to reclaim our energy back from patterns and behaviors that aren't serving our highest good. For

example, Marlene recently did this spell because she has a fixation on dairy products—or, as she puts it, she's a "cheeser"—despite the fact that she's lactose intolerant and eating dairy makes her feel like crap.

Since performing this spell, now, instead of Marlene feeling like cheese has an energetic hold over her, she's in control of the situation. Rather than being driven by cravings, it's much easier for Marlene to keep her focus on the higher good and betterment of herself (and the cow), which includes staying away from foods that don't serve her temple well.

INGREDIENTS

- 1 stick incense, such as dragon's blood, frankincense, or sage
- Water
- Vinegar
- Black taper candle
- White taper candle
- 1 lemon, peeled and halved
- Epsom salt
- Black pepper or black pepper oil
- Cayenne pepper

SUPPLIES

- Glass, for ritual use
- White plate, for ritual use
- Scissors, cleaned with water and a cloth before use

Burn the incense to clear your area and create a sacred space.

Pour the water into your ritual glass and add a few drops of vinegar. Place it on your altar. Light your black and white candles on your altar.

Place your lemon halves on the white plate. Open up the pair of scissors and place each point of the scissors into one of the lemon halves so that the scissors stand up. Sprinkle the Epsom salt, black pepper, and cayenne pepper onto the plate and lemons. Place the black candle on one side of the plate and the white candle on the other, then light the candles as you set your intention and visualize the things you would like to remove from your life.

Leave the water and plate on your altar for 9 days. To dispose of the lemons and candles, offer them at a trash can located on cemetery grounds to symbolize something that is now dead to your life experience.

✦ ✦ ✦

LOVE JAR

You will want to build and nurture your Love Jar over time because it's designed with the purpose of calling in a love that is sustainable and lasting. If you're not looking to bring new love into your life, this jar is also great for keeping and growing the love that you do have.

You can use your Love Jar to bring in romantic love, of course, but it's equally effective for any type of love. For example, if you want to build a more loving home or even a more loving business environment, you can create a Love Jar for that purpose. In fact, the two of us have actually never done a Love Jar with romance in mind, but we absolutely still have one.

And just a note here: Particularly when it comes to love, we frequently meet people who want to do *all* of the love rituals, all at once. Our best advice is: don't! Start with a love candle, then take a love bath (see Bath Ritual for Self-Love and Love, page 197), and, finally, go to a Love Jar. If you've done all of that and love still hasn't arrived, understand it's the universe's way of telling you there is still some work to be done before it's time for love to present itself. Remember, no matter how much you might desire something, the universe always has your best interests and timing in mind.

INGREDIENTS

- 1 stick incense, the variety of your choice
- 3 apples, halved (you will use 5 of the halves)
- Brown sugar, to sprinkle over the apples
- Cinnamon powder, to sprinkle over the apples
- 1 cup rosebuds, the color of your choice
- Peppermint oil
- 25 pennies
- Honey
- 4 white tea candles
- Red taper candle

SUPPLIES

Airtight jar, such as a mason jar	Red marker	White plate, for ritual use

Light the incense on your altar to clear your space. Cleanse your jar with water and set it aside to dry. Once the jar is dry, write your intention on it with the red marker, then place the jar on your altar.

Place the apple halves on the white plate, sprinkle them with sugar and cinnamon, and put the plate on your altar as an offering for spirit.

Over the next five days, add a bed of rosebuds, a drop of peppermint, 5 pennies, and a drizzle of honey each day.

For the first four days, follow this by lighting 1 tea candle on the lid of the jar as you reaffirm your intention. On the fifth day, burn the bottom of the red taper candle to melt a bit of the wax, then place the red taper candle on the lid of the jar, making sure it sticks to the top of your lid. Light the candlewick and set your intention. The spell is now complete.

Your jar can remain on your altar for as long as you choose, but should stay for a minimum of 5 days after you have finished burning the red taper candle. If you choose, you can remove the jar and put it in a meaningful location of your choice, such as in the bedroom or your business. If you want to dispose of the jar after your intention has been completed, you can dispose of it at a chapel or into a river or the ocean.

MONEY JAR

Among our client base, it seems that the majority of people gravitate toward love spells. But in our Potion Room, it's a different story: Everyone in there is all about the money spells!

The girls in our Potion Room constantly argue over who gets to work on the money candles. When we first heard this bartering taking place, we were concerned. Was everything okay? Were the girls in some sort of financial bind we were unaware of? But the answer was always the same: They already had love in their lives, so they didn't need to draw in more of that by working with the love magic. On the other hand, who can't do with a bit more money? Just recently, one of our girls won a $200 card for food at her local market and another won $600 on a lottery ticket. Both of them told us separately that they are sure it's because they worked on a large batch of money candles just before the prizes came their way. Sure, these aren't life-changing windfalls, but think of how this compounds when money spells become a part of your regular practice!

Every time we hear these conversations taking place in the Potion Room, they make us laugh. First of all, it speaks to how powerful magic is—and these girls know it, because they work with magic on a daily basis. For the purposes of this ritual, it points to how effective money spells are, whether you're looking to take care of something specific or, more generally, just want to generate more abundance in your life.

You can think of your Money Jar as a magical piggy bank. In our opinion, everyone should have one, regardless of their current financial status. Money Jars do attract abundance, but they also keep money in flow. Be aware, though, that this ritual is not a quick or fast-acting fix—after all, it calls for molasses, which is known for being slow moving.

Your Money Jar can stay on your altar for a long period of time, depending upon your intention—in fact, we recommend that you leave it be because the power and influence of Money Jars tends to get stronger over time. You can also reactivate your Money Jar at any time by lighting a new green taper candle on top of the jar's lid. We tend to reactivate ours when we are having a slow month at the store, for goal-setting, or when we are considering significant purchases.

You can hold on to your jar forever or release it whenever the time feels right. We release our Money Jars into the ocean, but banks are also a perfect place to offer up their energy.

INGREDIENTS

1 stick incense of your choice

1 box rice or oats

9 cloves

21 dimes

3 basil leaves

3 teaspoons molasses

2 white tealight candles

1 green taper candle

SUPPLIES

Airtight jar, such as a mason jar

Pencil

Piece of brown paper

Light the incense to clear your space.

Cleanse your jar with water and allow it to dry, then place the jar on your altar.

Write the intention for your jar in pencil on the brown piece of paper. Be as specific as possible. When you are finished, place the paper in the jar.

Over the course of three days, add a bed of rice or oats, 3 cloves, 7 dimes, 1 basil leaf, and 1 teaspoon of molasses to the jar per day. Think of a lasagna as you layer each of these ingredients. After you layer the ingredients, light 1 white tealight candle on the lid of your jar for the first and second day, setting your intention as you light the candle.

After you have added the third layer on the third day, light the bottom of the green taper candle so that it melts a bit of the wax. Place the bottom of the candle on top of the lid of your jar, making sure it sticks to the top of your lid. Then, light the candlewick and set your intention.

You can hold on to your Money Jar and continue to reactivate it over time. Or, if you prefer, once your request or intention has been fulfilled, you can offer your jar at a crossroads or a bank, bury it in a safe spot away from your home, or release it into the ocean.

✦ ✦ ✦

STEP INTO YOUR ABUNDANCE SHOE RITUAL

There was a time when you could be sure that every single shoe we owned had a dime in it. When we tried on new shoes, the salespeople would often kindly let us know that we had a dime stuck to our foot. "Hmmm, how did that get there?" we would respond, feigning surprise.

This is a powerful ritual because you will actually feel the dime in your shoe as you walk through your daily life, which serves the purpose of constantly bringing your awareness back to your intention. If you get tired of feeling the dimes after a while (like we did), you can get inserts for the purpose of more comfortably stashing dimes in your shoes. Sometimes you gotta do what you gotta do when it comes to magic!

INGREDIENTS

2 dimes

2 yellow rose petals

1 stick of incense (we recommend dragon's blood, mugwort, sage, or yerba santa)

SUPPLIES

1 small white bowl, for ritual use

1 pair of shoes you wear frequently

Place the dimes and rose petals in the white bowl on your altar, then cleanse your space with incense as you hold your intention in your mind's eye. Wait for three days and, on the third day, remove the dimes and rose petals from your altar.

Place 1 rose petal under the sole of each shoe. Place 1 dime heads up on top of the sole of the left shoe; the left side of the body is associated with receiving, consciousness, and awareness. Place the other dime tails up on top of the sole of your right shoe; the right side of the body is associated with giving and is where power and strength reside. The tails-up coin on this side also represents protection (imagine how certain animals lift their tails before attack).

Every time you wear these shoes from this moment forward, each step you take with your left foot will bring love and riches. Each step you take with your right foot will send love and riches out to others, while also guarding and protecting you from those who do not deserve your gifts.

✦ ✦ ✦

BUSINESS MONEY BAG

Have you ever thought about what the bells at churches actually signify? For religious purposes, bells call in gods, spirits, or angels.

Since bells draw the attention of those energies that protect and assist us, we place Money Bags on the doors of our business so that each time the bell rings, it draws spirit's attention in our direction. Ethereal assistance aside, the ring of the bell serves as a constant reminder of our intention to draw in money.

It's funny, because even though we've had these money bags hanging on our business doors for more than a decade now, only one customer has ever noticed. "Why do you have money hanging on your door here?" she asked. "Aren't you afraid someone's going to steal it?"

We weren't . . . until that moment, at least!

If you don't have a doorknob on the front door of your business, you can also place the ingredients included in this ritual into a bowl, and place the bowl behind your door.

INGREDIENTS

- 1 basil leaf
- 1 cinnamon stick
- 3 dimes
- 7 nickels
- 9 pennies
- 5 quarters
- White candle
- Red candle

SUPPLIES

- Small bowl, for ritual use
- Bag or sack with a drawstring
- Small bell

Put the basil leaf, cinnamon stick, dimes, nickels, pennies, and quarters in a bowl, then put the bowl on the center of your altar. Place the white candle in front of the bowl to represent light, purity, and the angelic realm. As you light the white candle, visualize your bowl being blessed. Place the red candle directly behind your bowl to represent protection. As you light the red candle, visualize the success of your business and allow a sense of gratitude to wash over you.

Leave the bowl on your altar for 3 days, lighting the candles when you are present or comfortable with them being lit.

On the fourth day, transfer the ingredients from your bowl into the bag. Loop the bell onto the drawstring and tie the bag to the doorknob of your business. Know that every time your door opens or closes, the bell is calling to your spirit guides, sending a message of protection and abundance out to the universe on your business's behalf. The Business Money Bag can remain on your door from that point forward.

✦ ✦ ✦

SWEETEN UP YOUR BUSINESS

The Sweeten Up Your Business floor wash is specifically designed for new businesses. We do this ritualistic wash every time we open up a new HOI location.

We first used this spell when we took over a space downstairs from the original HOI. It was a dark, dingy room that had been formerly occupied by a psychic reader for more than twenty years. We needed more space because we were expanding our classes, and the proximity of this place was perfect. Not perfect was the fact that it had a ton of stagnant, heavy, dark energy.

It was grimy in the physical sense, too. Okay, let's be honest: It was hideous. Like, really, really bad. It was clear that this place hadn't been cleaned in *any* way—literally or figuratively—in the past twenty years.

Still, we knew that we could clean the place up and transform it into a clean, warm space in which to host our classes.

To physically clean the space and lift the energy, we created this spell. We used the candy to sweeten up the space and bring in love. We literally threw bucket upon bucket of candy into the room. Basically, we exorcised the place by candy. We did this day after day for twenty-one days straight. We also prayed, meditated, and visualized white light and light energy.

Chances are, you won't have to clear the type of heavy energy we did before opening up your new business. But, even if you do, this spell works wonders. It will clear away any lingering stagnation, the candy draws in clients with its sweetness, and the coins bring in abundance.

INGREDIENTS

¼ to ½ bottle Florida Water, depending upon the size of your space

Bucket of water from the faucet

Candy, individually wrapped

Coins

Dried corn kernels

Sweep the floor, then mop it with the Florida Water and the bucket of water. Once the floor is clean, throw the candy, coins, and corn kernels on the floor and sweep them around the room so that they are dispersed throughout the building. Allow them to sit for 24 hours.

Once 24 hours have passed, sweep the candy, coins, and corn kernels outside the front door of your business and leave them there to energetically draw customers in.

BLESSINGS FOR NEW CONTRACTS OR PARTNERSHIPS

This blessing can be used on contracts of all kinds, for anything from buying a new home to custody agreements to entering into a new partnership or venture. As you perform this ritual, ask that anything included in the contract that doesn't serve your best interests be brought to your attention. Then notice what happens.

If, for example, you perform this blessing and then get an email to cancel the contract, don't force it through. If you are signing a loan that suddenly asks for an additional five thousand dollars, understand that it's a warning sign.

We've been taking our contracts to the altar since long before HOI was born, but the most memorable results of a contract blessing happened when we leased our North Hollywood HOI location. We were super excited to lease this particular place because it's the building where the original *Karate Kid* movie was filmed. We *really* wanted to set up shop there and soak in some of the cobra energy. At the time we viewed it, the location had been vacant for a couple of years. We verbally negotiated the price and terms with the owner and were feeling good when we put the contract on the altar.

The next day, we removed the contract from our altar to sign it. That's when we noticed a clause on the last page stating that the rent would increase significantly every year over a five-year period. This was *not* part of our discussion. We pulled out of the deal immediately. The owner was persistent, though, and in the end, he let us name our own price, which resulted in a significantly lower monthly rate, and no

annual increases. To this day, we feel like it was spirit's way of whispering, "You can do better." Pay attention to what spirit whispers to you.

INGREDIENTS

- 1 cup freshly brewed coffee
- 1 stick incense of your choice
- Contract
- Small bowl of water
- White candle

SUPPLIES

- Pencil
- Piece of brown paper

Place the cup of coffee on your altar as an offering for your ancestors. Light the incense to purify the space and bring in the energy of the air, fire, and earth elements. Write your intention on the piece of brown paper in pencil.

Place the contract and piece of brown paper in the center of your altar, then place the bowl of water on top of the contract and paper. Not only does the water protect the candle, but it also brings an element of purity to your contract. Place your candle in the bowl of water to represent spirit and white light. Set your intention for your partnership or endeavor as you light the candle.

When the candle has burned down, light the end of the brown paper and then place it in the bowl of water to seal your intention.

Once you have finished your spell, take the bowl with the melted candle and burned paper to a road that has four corners and dispose of it at one of the corners. This represents a clear road for your new journey.

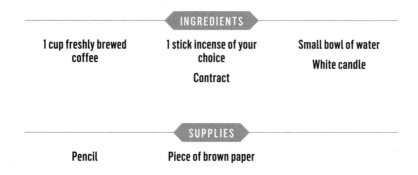

BLESSINGS FOR MONEY AND ABUNDANCE

We've been asked more than once why our money smells like Santa Claus. This ritual answers that question: Most of our money is sprinkled with peppermint oil.

This spell is so much fun because, in addition to creating money that smells like Santa Claus, it also makes you *feel* a little bit like Santa Claus. Not only will this ritual bring abundance into your own life, but it will also bring abundance to anyone whose hand touches your blessed money. For that reason, we love doing this ritual with kids. Not only does it teach them that creating a life of abundance is possible and okay, but it also demonstrates lessons in generosity and paying it forward.

If you'd like, you can swap out the bills in this spell with checks or anything else you use as currency. Notice how much better you feel about spending money when you know that you are spreading blessings with each dollar that leaves your hand. It's particularly gratifying to perform this blessing with money that is being donated to charity.

INGREDIENTS

Cinnamon chips or a crushed cinnamon stick

Citrine or ruby crystal (your choice)

Pyrite crystal

Bills (however many and of whatever amount you choose)

Peppermint oil

Green candle

SUPPLIES

Large bowl, for ritual use

Place the cinnamon chips and crystals into a bowl. Anoint each bill with peppermint oil, then place the bills in your bowl, on top of the crystals and cinnamon.

Light the candle on your altar as you visualize the money in the bowl creating more money with each hand that it touches. Know that every dollar you spend will bless the person that touches it next and that the blessing will be sent back to you ten times over. Once you have finished this visualization, take a moment to express gratitude for all of the abundance in your life.

Keep the bills with you to spend when the time comes. As you spend each one of them, recite the following mantra in your head: *I release abundance to the next and return it to me with much success.*

BLESSING AND GRATITUDE RITUAL FOR ANCESTORS

The books used in this blessing represent a staircase leading up to the gates of heaven. With this blessing, you are lifting your ancestors up to those gates.

We do this blessing *all* the time. In fact, next to Alex's Anxiety Bath (see page 207), this is probably the most frequently performed ritual in our home. On holidays, all of our ancestors get fed before we do as part of this blessing. On birthdays, ancestors are served up their favorite cake on our altar along with this blessing. Regularly, we brew our ancestors coffee and serve it with this blessing. We also make a point of doing this ritual anytime an intention comes to fruition or we are feeling grateful to the spirits that protect us. We consider this blessing our ancestors' bonus for a job well done, and it's also a beautiful way of connecting with our loved ones who have passed. You can use this blessing for all of these reasons or for whatever else moves you.

This is also a beautiful blessing to perform when someone you love passes over. We know so many people who have found comfort and connection through the act of creating a physical space for the souls that protect and guide them. This blessing does exactly that.

INGREDIENTS

1 stick incense of your choice

Cross, rosary, or sacred personal item that represents your ancestors

Picture of your ancestors

Food offering of your choice, such as bread, fruit, or one of your ancestor's favorite meals

1 glass of water, poured into a glass reserved for ritual use

Shot glass of white vodka or coffee

2 candles in glass candleholders

6 books

SUPPLIES

White plate, for ritual use

Light the incense to clear your space. Set all of the items except for the 6 books on your altar. You may remove the food offering after the first day or leave it on your altar for the duration of your ritual or for however long feels right to you.

Light 1 of the candles on your altar as you focus on gratitude to your ancestors. You will continue lighting that candle over the course of the next 6 days until it burns down, at which point you will light the second candle. On the second day, place a book under your candle and focus on your gratitude as you light the candle again. For the next 5 days, place 1 additional book under the candle per day, until you have placed all 6 books under the candle. Symbolically, you are providing your ancestors with light for 7 days as you raise them higher and higher off the Earth plane with your gratitude for their assistance.

Throughout this 7-day period, continue talking to your ancestors, both when you are at your altar and when you are not, asking them to connect with you and show you signs. This is an incredibly powerful ritual, so don't be surprised if odd things happen. Your TV or radio might turn on or off. You might catch a whiff of your grandma's perfume or discover that a white butterfly flits into your car. There will be some movement, so don't be afraid. Your ancestors are just saying hello and thank you in response to your blessing, letting you know that they are listening, and acknowledging the open channel you have created. If you notice any messages, pay attention, acknowledge them, and say thank you.

On the seventh day, allow your candle to continue burning until it has completely burned down. Your ritual is now complete.

✦ ✦ ✦

CHAPTER SEVEN

INTUITION-LED RITUALS

HERE'S WHERE YOU GET TO REALLY TAKE YOUR INTUITION OUT FOR A SPIN. IN THE rituals that follow, you will see a listing of base ingredients. These serve as the foundation of the ritual. After that, you will see additional lists of suggestions for herbs, oils, and crystals to choose among. It is these elements that add the specificity to your magic. Don't think about which to choose—just notice what pops into your mind and go with that. By this point, it should go without saying that if an ingredient that *isn't* included on the list of suggestions comes to mind, you should absolutely use that ingredient.

When you have finished the ritual, flip to the appendix (page 248) to see what the ingredients you've chosen symbolize. Take note of how closely it matches your situation and intention.

CANDLE MAGIC FOR CONFIDENCE AND STRENGTH

Lavender candles symbolize inner and emotional healing. When you heal yourself emotionally, you build up and are able to bring more confidence and strength into the world. As the layers of emotional scars and residue melt away along with the candle, you will become more in touch with your lioness energy. With that in mind, conjure up the lion as you perform this ritual. Visualize yourself cultivating that energy within—or, more accurately, acknowledging the lioness energy that is already within you.

This is a great ritual to perform as preparation for walking into a situation in any area of your life in which you need to stand your ground or withstand pressure.

For extra potency and amplification, begin this ritual on a Tuesday to match the energy of the candle magic.

BASE INGREDIENTS

Lavender candle	1 bay leaf	Coconut shavings

HERBS / GOODS (CHOOSE 1 TO 3)

Lemon peel	Mugwort	Thyme

OILS (CHOOSE 1 TO 3)

Eucalyptus	Lavender	Mandarin

CRYSTALS (CHOOSE 1 STONE)

Beryl

Chrysocolla

Tiger's eye

OFFERINGS (CHOOSE 1 TO 4)

Bread

Coconut

Flowers

Eggs

SUPPLIES

Small bowl filled with water to hold your candle
(optional, if your candle is not held in a glass container)

Create a sacred space by clearing your mind of everything except for your intention. Say a prayer to your guides, ancestors, or the deity of your choice.

Cleanse your candle from dirt, dust, and any energy it may be holding by using a soft cloth that is lightly dabbed with soap and water. You can also use alcohol or holy water if you prefer. Trim the wick when you are finished cleansing.

Gather the base ingredients, herbs, oils, and crystal of your choice and meditate over them to infuse them with your intention. Chop your herbs into very small pieces.

To anoint your candle, tilt the bottle of oil (or oils) onto your fingertip, then rub your fingertip around the top of the candle, into the wax. If you want to bring something into your life, rub the oil clockwise; to reverse or release something or for protection, rub the oil counterclockwise. Sprinkle a pinch of the herbs over the oil. Less is always more, because too much product can smother your candle.

Place the offering of your choice on your altar as you express gratitude to your ancestors for their assistance in facilitating your intention. Put your anointed candle in a small bowl of water and place it on your altar. Depending on its size, you can place the crystal of your choice either in the bowl of water holding the candle or next to the candle on your altar. If you wish, you can also write your intention on a piece of paper and place that note under the bowl holding your candle.

As you light your candle, hold your intention at the front of your mind's eye and meditate on that vision. When you feel ready, express gratitude to your ancestors, spirit guides, spirits, and all of the beings acting on your behalf.

If you can't leave your candle burning, snuff it out when you feel ready. Do not blow it out, because you don't want to blow away your intention. Whenever possible, try to stay in ritual by lighting and snuffing out your candle around the same time each day until the candle is finished. Every time you relight your candle, you begin your ritual anew. This means you will want to reset and visualize your intention with each lighting. Continue doing this until the candle has completely burned down.

Once your candle has burned down, you can keep the glass container that held it on your altar as a reminder if you wish. You might want to fill it with an item that reminds you of your intention. If you would prefer to dispose of the candle, deposit it in a trash can at a church or temple, gym, holistic center, hospital, or in nature. Choose the location that best matches the energy of your intention and remain in a state of gratitude as you deposit the candle.

✦ ✦ ✦

CANDLE MAGIC FOR PEACE AND HARMONY

The blue candle in this spell symbolizes serenity, calmness, and well-being. The ritual is a double-whammy because not only does this candle help usher in peace and harmony, but it also removes feelings of anger and fear. Blue is associated with the throat chakra, so when you perform this ritual, you are healing and strengthening the ways in which you express (or, perhaps in this case, do not express) yourself and your emotions.

For extra potency and amplification, begin this ritual on a Sunday to match the energy of the candle magic.

BASE INGREDIENTS

Blue candle

Coconut shavings

Myrrh (in your choice of resin, oil, or herb form)

HERBS (CHOOSE 1 TO 4)

Chamomile

Rosemary

Thyme

Tobacco, extracted from a cigar

OILS (CHOOSE 1 TO 2)

Lavender

Ylang-ylang

CRYSTALS (CHOOSE 1 STONE)

Amethyst

Shungite

Sodalite

OFFERINGS (CHOOSE 1 TO 4)

Bread

Coconut

Flowers

Eggs

SUPPLIES

Small bowl filled with water to hold your candle (optional, if your candle is not held in a glass container)

Begin creating a sacred space by clearing your mind of everything except for your intention. Say a prayer to your guides, ancestors, or the deity of your choice.

Cleanse your candle from dirt, dust, and any energy it may be holding by using a soft cloth that is lightly dabbed with soap and water. You can also use alcohol or holy water if you prefer. Trim the wick when you are finished cleansing.

Gather the herbs, oils, and crystal of your choice and meditate over them to infuse them with your intention. Chop your herbs into very small pieces.

To anoint your candle, tilt the bottle of oil (or oils) onto your fingertip, then rub your fingertip around the top of the candle, into the wax. If you want to bring something into your life, rub the oil clockwise; to reverse or release something or for protection, rub the oil counterclockwise. Sprinkle a pinch of the herbs over the oil. Less is always more, because too much product can smother your candle.

Place the offering of your choice on your altar, expressing gratitude to your ancestors for their assistance in facilitating your intention. Put your anointed candle in a small bowl of water and place it on your altar. Depending on its size, you can place the crystal of your choice either in the bowl of water holding the candle or next to the candle on your altar. If you wish, you can also write your intention on a piece of paper and place that note under the bowl holding your candle.

As you light your candle, hold your intention at the front of your mind's eye and meditate on that vision. When you feel ready, express gratitude to your ancestors, spirit guides, spirits, and all of the beings acting on your behalf.

If you can't leave your candle burning, snuff it out when you feel ready. Do not blow it out, because you don't want to blow away your intention. Whenever possible, try to stay in ritual by lighting and snuffing out your candle around the same time each day until the candle has finished. Every time you relight your candle, you begin your ritual anew. This means you will want to reset and visualize your intention with each lighting. Continue doing this until the candle has completely burned down.

Once your candle has burned down, you can keep the glass container that held it on your altar as a reminder if you wish. You might want to fill it with an item that reminds you of your intention. If you would prefer to dispose of the candle, deposit it in a trash can at a church or temple, gym, holistic center, hospital, or in nature. Choose the location that best matches the energy of your intention and remain in a state of gratitude as you deposit the candle.

✦ ✦ ✦

CANDLE MAGIC FOR HEART HEALING

If you are on the cusp of a breakup or in the throes of dealing with one, this is the spell for you.

Green candles stimulate renewal and heart healing. This candle spell offers a way to nurture yourself into deep healing rather than just slapping a Band-Aid on the immediate pain of heartbreak. All Band-Aids do—especially when they're placed on the heart—is leave more work for us to do in the future.

Whenever someone comes into the shop and says they keep dating the same type of guy or girl over and over again even though they want to draw in someone different, we lead them toward healing the heart. This kind of repetitive behavior is a sure sign that the same patterns are being repeated, resulting in the same pain over and over again. One of the basic laws of the universe is that we have to let go before we can move forward. So often, people come back to us after burning this candle to tell us they didn't even realize how much old heartbreak they were carrying with them.

For extra potency and amplification, begin this spell on a Sunday to match the energy of the candle magic.

BASE INGREDIENTS

Green candle	**Oregano**	**Red rose petals**

HERBS (CHOOSE 1 TO 3)

Parsley	**Rosemary**	**Thyme**

OILS (CHOOSE 1 TO 3)

Bergamot

Sweet orange

Vanilla

CRYSTALS (CHOOSE 1 STONE)

Green calcite

Jade

Rose quartz

OFFERINGS (CHOOSE 1 TO 4)

Bread

Coconut

Flowers

Eggs

SUPPLIES

Small bowl filled with water to hold your candle (optional, if your candle is not held in a glass container)

Begin creating a sacred space by clearing your mind of everything except for your intention. Say a prayer to your guides, ancestors, or the deity of your choice.

Cleanse your candle from dirt, dust, and any energy it may be holding by using a soft cloth that is lightly dabbled with soap and water. You can also use alcohol or holy water if you prefer. Trim the wick when you are finished cleansing.

Gather the flower petals, herbs, oils, and crystal of your choice and meditate over them to infuse them with your intention. Chop your petals and herbs into very small pieces.

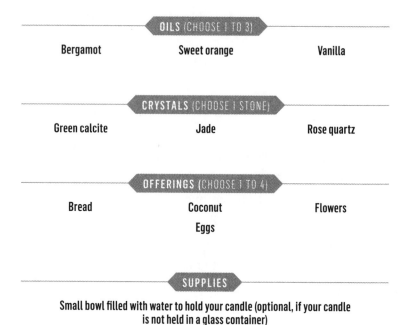

To anoint your candle, tilt the bottle of oil (or oils) onto your fingertip, then rub your fingertip around the top of the candle, into the wax. If you want to bring something into your life, rub the oil clockwise; to reverse or release something or for protection, rub the oil counterclockwise. Sprinkle a pinch of the herbs over the oil. Less is always more, because too much product can smother your candle.

Place the offering of your choice on your altar, expressing gratitude to your ancestors for their assistance in facilitating your intention. Put your anointed candle in a small bowl of water and place it on your altar. Depending on its size, you can place the crystal of your choice either in the bowl of water holding the candle or next to the candle on your altar. If you wish, you can also write your intention on a piece of paper and place that note under the bowl holding your candle.

As you light your candle, hold your intention at the front of your mind's eye and meditate on that vision. When you feel ready, express gratitude to your ancestors, spirit guides, spirits, and all of the beings acting on your behalf.

If you can't leave your candle burning, snuff it out when you feel ready. Do not blow it out, because you don't want to blow away your intention. Whenever possible, try to stay in ritual by lighting and snuffing out your candle around the same time each day until the candle has finished. Every time you relight your candle, you begin your ritual anew. This means you will want to reset and visualize your intention with each lighting. Continue doing this until the candle has completely burned down.

Once your candle has burned down, you can keep the glass container that held it on your altar as a reminder if you wish. You might want to fill it with an item that reminds you of your intention. If you would prefer to dispose of the candle, deposit it in a trash can at a church or temple, gym, holistic center, hospital, or in nature. Choose the location that best matches the energy of your intention and remain in a state of gratitude as you deposit the candle.

✦ ✦ ✦

BATH RITUAL FOR SELF-LOVE AND LOVE

When people come in looking for a love ritual, they often become impatient about the self-love part of this spell. They want to hurry up and get on to the main attraction already—the exciting part of love! What they don't understand is that self-love is a necessary part of finding the right person to love you. It's not possible to accept the unconditional love of another person until you first love yourself. Both of us have learned this the hard way.

This ritual might sound like it's for a specific purpose, but in our mind it falls firmly into the preventive magical care category. Finding true love doesn't happen in a single moment in time. It requires a lot of growth, work, and acceptance to get to that point. You have to accept yourself for who you are before you can expect someone else to, and that acceptance often requires a journey that takes some time. Love attracts love; once you love yourself for who you are, others will, too.

The way we see it, if you're going to do hard internal work like this, you might as well do it while soaking in champagne, honey, and rose petals. The decadence of this bath provides the opportunity to do something we should all do on a more regular basis: celebrate ourselves! Soaking in champagne, in particular, will leave you feeling effervescent and heighten all of your senses. As you soak, you can reflect on all of the hard work it took those little bees to make the honey and how sweet the final result is.

Like Candle Magic for Heart Healing, we recommend this ritual bath for anyone who keeps attracting the same person over and over again. By learning to love yourself, you will open the door for something new to come in.

For extra potency and amplification, perform this spell on a Friday to match the energy of the intention. We recommend performing bath rituals of any variety right before you go to bed. You don't want to go back into the world after cleansing your energy. It's time to relax, absorb the energies of the infusion you've made, and detach from daily life.

BASE INGREDIENTS

Red or pink candle

½ bottle of champagne

1 teaspoon honey (or molasses, if you prefer)

FLOWERS (CHOOSE 1 TO 4)

Petals of forget-me-nots

Petals of jasmine

Petals of red rose

Petals of sunflower

OILS (CHOOSE 1 TO 4)

Geranium

Patchouli

Rosemary

Vanilla

CRYSTALS (CHOOSE 1 STONE)

Chrysoprase

Garnet

Kunzite

Rose quartz

OFFERINGS (CHOOSE 1 TO 3)

Apple

Avocado

Cherry

SUPPLIES

Large bowl, for ritual use

Place the candle on your altar and light it as you hold your intention in your mind's eye. Put your offerings on your altar and express gratitude to your ancestors, spirit guides, and the deities that resonate with you.

Remain in a state of intention and prayer as you begin preparing your ingredients. Pour the champagne into a bowl and add in the honey (or molasses) and flower petals. Mix the ingredients together with your hands. Drop in the oil (conservatively for the sake of your plumbing!) and place your crystal in the bowl.

Take the bowl to your altar and infuse it with your intention. You may leave it there for whatever amount of time feels right to you.

When you are ready to take your bath or shower, remove the crystal and place it on your altar. Leave the candle burning as you take the bowl into the bathroom with you. Place the bowl either next to the tub, or on the floor of the shower if you choose to perform this ritual as a shower.

Ritual baths are generally taken in cooler-temperature water because it's more calming; if you are taking a shower, begin with warm water, then switch to lukewarm or cold when you are ready to actively perform the ritual.

Cleanse your physical body first—use soap, shampoo, and perform all of your normal cleansing practices. Once you have done that, you can turn your attention to your emotional and spiritual bodies. When you are ready to begin the active ritual, hold the bowl above your head and pray, recite your intention, thank your angels, spirit guides, or ancestors, whatever feels right to you. Tilt the bowl and allow the mixture to wash over you. Sweep the mixture over your body, visualizing as you go. As you sweep, you will effectively remove the herbs from your body; this symbolizes removing those things that don't serve you. Visualize all of the things you are washing away—negativity, fear, or any baggage that you might be holding on to unnecessarily. As you let go, you are simultaneously nourishing the new skin that is rising to the surface. As you release, you also receive. Allow yourself to see what you want to activate, or see white light beaming out from around your entire body. Breathe in clarity as you go.

When you are finished, rinse off with water, then towel yourself dry. You may still have some lingering herbs on you, and that's okay. When you dress after your bath, try to use colors that are associated with the ritual you have just performed, whether it's through your pajamas, a hair turban, or the sheets you lie in. The energetic power of color will help keep you in your ritual. (For more on color, see page 111.)

✦ ✦ ✦

BATH RITUAL FOR HEALING AND BALANCE

So many of us struggle with how to balance the various areas of our lives. Work, family, relationships, and self-care—it can feel like a constant, complex juggling act. We wish we had time for a 90-minute massage or 1-hour meditation on a regular basis, but we usually don't. So, instead, both of us frequently take this bath to avoid overwhelm.

This ritual bath is a great 15-minute reprieve in those times when it feels like there's no room for you in your own life. The oils such as sandalwood and cypress offer earth energy with which to ground, while the eucalyptus simultaneously lifts and brightens. It's also a great bath for kids when they feel overwhelmed or require calming. If you would prefer not to perform the actual ritual on them, the ingredients alone will soothe and relax.

The energy of this ritual is best aligned with Sundays for maximum impact and potency but, particularly in this case, you should take it whenever you need some relief and relaxation.

BASE INGREDIENTS

- Blue candle
- Ground eggshell (cascarilla)
- Lavender
- Water (preferably holy water) or goat's milk

HERBS (CHOOSE 1 TO 3)

- Bay leaf
- Chamomile
- Eucalyptus

OILS (CHOOSE 1 TO 3)

Cypress	Lime	Sandalwood

CRYSTALS (CHOOSE 1 STONE)

Bloodstone	Blue apatite	Turquoise

OFFERINGS (CHOOSE 1 TO 3)

Bouquet of flowers	Bread	White pumpkin
	Eggs	

SUPPLIES

Large bowl, for ritual use

Place the candle on your altar and light it as you hold your intention in your mind's eye. Put your offerings on your altar and express gratitude to your ancestors, spirit guides, and the deities that resonate with you.

Remain in a state of intention and prayer as you begin preparing your ingredients. Steep the lavender and additional herbs of your choice in hot water, then drain the herbs, placing them in a bowl and discarding the hot water. Add the cascarilla and holy water or goat's milk, drop in the oil (conservatively for the sake of your plumbing!), then place your crystal in the bowl.

Take the bowl to your altar and infuse it with your intention. You may leave it there for whatever amount of time feels right to you.

When you are ready to take your bath or shower, remove the crystal and place it on your altar. Leave the candle burning as you take the bowl into the bathroom with you. Place the bowl either next

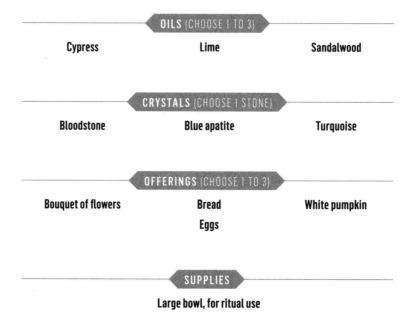

to the tub, or on the floor of the shower if you choose to perform this ritual as a shower.

Ritual baths are generally taken in cooler-temperature water because it's more calming; if you are taking a shower, begin with warm water, then switch to lukewarm or cold when you are ready to actively perform the ritual.

Cleanse your physical body first—use soap, shampoo, and perform all of your normal cleansing practices. Once you have done that, you can turn your attention to your emotional and spiritual bodies. When you are ready to begin the active ritual, hold the bowl above your head and pray, recite your intention, thank your angels, spirit guides, or ancestors, whatever feels right to you. Tilt the bowl and allow the mixture to wash over you. Sweep the mixture over your body, visualizing as you go. As you sweep, you will effectively remove the herbs from your body; this symbolizes removing those things that don't serve you. Visualize all of the things you are washing away—negativity, fear, or any baggage that you might be holding on to unnecessarily. As you let go, you are simultaneously nourishing the new skin that is rising to the surface. As you release, you also receive. Allow yourself to see what you want to activate, or see white light beaming out from around your entire body. Breathe in clarity as you go.

When you are finished, rinse off with water, then towel yourself dry. You may still have some lingering herbs on you, and that's okay. When you dress after your bath, try to use colors that are associated with the ritual you have just performed, whether it's through your pajamas, a hair turban, or the sheets you lie in. The energetic power of color will help keep you in your ritual.

✦ ✦ ✦

RITUAL BATH TO PURIFY AND RELEASE NEGATIVITY (AKA ALEX'S ANXIETY BATH)

Alex takes this bath a lot, because she tends to run on the anxious side. When left unchecked, this anxiety can start to feel confining, as if she's dragging a heavy weight along with her everywhere she goes. She always emerges from this bath feeling lighter, more open, and more centered.

In addition to being an incredible antidote to anxiety, this bath is also a great go-to in those moments when you are grappling with stress, depression, or recurring nightmares. It brings about a sense of tranquility and uplifts the heavy energy or emotions that can build up in all of us.

This is what's known as a white bath because, as you'll see, it includes a lot of white ingredients, including the milk base. The feeling of milk on your body is calming in and of itself, almost as if you are being coated in protection. It's energetically similar to the physical sensation of getting clean after having mud splattered all over you.

The energy of this ritual is best aligned with Saturdays for maximum impact and potency but, particularly in this case, you should take it whenever you need some relief and relaxation.

BASE INGREDIENTS

White or black candle	Egg white Milk	Water

FLOWERS (CHOOSE 1 TO 3)

Petals of white carnations	Petals of white roses	Sage

OILS (CHOOSE 1 TO 3)

Camphor	Lemon	White copal

CRYSTALS (CHOOSE 1 STONE)

Amethyst	Clear quartz	Selenite

OFFERINGS (CHOOSE 1 TO 3)

Coffee	Lemons	Tobacco

SUPPLIES

Large bowl, for ritual use

Place the candle on your altar and light it as you hold your intention in your mind's eye. Put your offerings on your altar and express gratitude to your ancestors, spirit guides, and the deities that resonate with you.

Remain in a state of intention and prayer as you begin preparing your ingredients. Place the flower petals, egg white, milk, and water in a bowl, then drop in the oil (conservatively for the sake of your plumbing!). Place your crystal in the bowl along with the ingredients.

Take the bowl to your altar and infuse it with your intention. You may leave it there for whatever amount of time feels right to you.

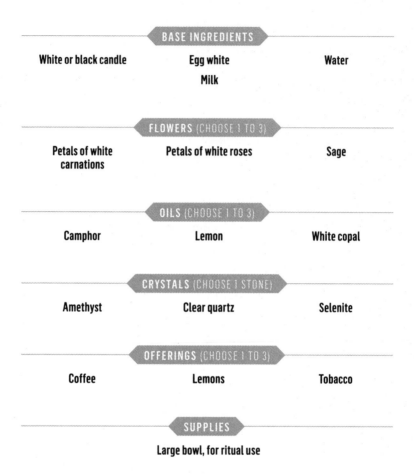

When you are ready to take your bath or shower, remove the crystal and place it on your altar. Leave the candle burning as you take the bowl into the bathroom with you. Place the bowl either next to the tub, or on the floor of the shower if you choose to perform this ritual as a shower.

Ritual baths are generally taken in cooler-temperature water because it's more calming; if you are taking a shower, begin with warm water, then switch to lukewarm or cold when you are ready to actively perform the ritual.

Cleanse your physical body first—use soap, shampoo, and perform all of your normal cleansing practices. Once you have done that, you can turn your attention to your emotional and spiritual bodies. When you are ready to begin the active ritual, hold the bowl above your head and pray, recite your intention, thank your angels, spirit guides, or ancestors, whatever feels right to you. Tilt the bowl and allow the mixture to wash over you. Sweep the mixture over your body, visualizing as you go. As you sweep, you will effectively remove the herbs from your body; this symbolizes removing those things that don't serve you. Visualize all of the things you are washing away—negativity, fear, or any baggage that you might be holding on to unnecessarily. As you let go, you are simultaneously nourishing the new skin that is rising to the surface. As you release, you also receive. Allow yourself to see what you want to activate, or see white light beaming out from around your entire body. Breathe in clarity as you go.

When you are finished, rinse off with water, then towel yourself dry. You may still have some lingering herbs on you, and that's okay. Maintain the white energy of the bath and its essence of purity by dressing in all white after you bathe.

PROTECTION BATH

There are certain rituals we perform on a regular basis—kind of like magical preventive medicine. The Protection Bath is one of those rituals. Here's the thing: The truth of the matter is that, as you walk through life, you just don't know what sort of energy you might encounter. We're not talking about hexes or curses or anything like that, but the more mundane ill will that each of us has been on the receiving end of at some point in our lives, often in the form of jealousy or envy.

The Protection Bath serves as a shield and purification from this type of energy. Once all of that energy is cleared from your field, you'll find that your path becomes much clearer and easier to navigate. This bath is particularly powerful because beer activates the other ingredients to maximize your protection.

To amplify and add potency to this bath, perform it on a Tuesday as the energy of that day is most aligned with this intention.

BASE INGREDIENTS

Black or white candle

1 can beer

2 tablespoons salt

Water

HERBS (CHOOSE 1 TO 4)

Anise

Clove

Garlic

Sage

OILS (CHOOSE 1 TO 4)

Basil

Frankincense

Myrrh

Pepper

CRYSTALS (CHOOSE 1 STONE)

Apache tears

Black obsidian

Black tourmaline

Labradorite

OFFERINGS (CHOOSE 1 TO 4)

Aloe plant

Black salt

Corn

Papaya

SUPPLIES

Small bowl, for ritual use

Place the candle on your altar and light it as you hold your intention in your mind's eye. Put your offerings on your altar and express gratitude to your ancestors, spirit guides, and the deities that resonate with you.

Remain in a state of intention and prayer as you begin preparing your ingredients. Steep the herbs of your choice in hot water, then drain the herbs and place them in a bowl. Add the beer, salt, and water, drop in the oil (conservatively for the sake of your plumbing!), and place your crystal in the bowl.

Take the bowl to your altar and infuse it with your intention. You may leave it there for whatever amount of time feels right to you.

When you are ready to take your bath or shower, remove the crystal and place it on your altar. Leave the candle burning as you take the bowl into the bathroom with you. Place the bowl either next

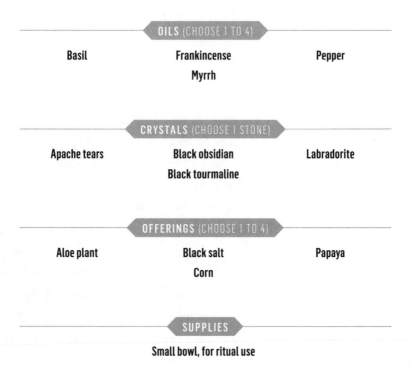

to the tub, or on the floor of the shower if you choose to perform this ritual as a shower.

Ritual baths are generally taken in cooler-temperature water because it's more calming; if you are taking a shower, begin with warm water, then switch to lukewarm or cold when you are ready to actively perform the ritual.

Cleanse your physical body first—use soap, shampoo, and perform all of your normal cleansing practices. Once you have done that, you can turn your attention to your emotional and spiritual bodies. When you are ready to begin the active ritual, hold the bowl above your head and pray, recite your intention, thank your angels, spirit guides, or ancestors, whatever feels right to you. Tilt the bowl and allow the mixture to wash over you. Sweep the mixture over your body, visualizing as you go. As you sweep, you will effectively remove the herbs from your body; this symbolizes removing those things that don't serve you. Visualize all of the things you are washing away—negativity, fear, or any baggage that you might be holding on to unnecessarily. As you let go, you are simultaneously nourishing the new skin that is rising to the surface. As you release, you also receive. Allow yourself to see what you want to activate, or see white light beaming out from around your entire body. Breathe in clarity as you go.

When you are finished, rinse off with water, then towel yourself dry. You may still have some lingering herbs on you, and that's okay. When you dress after your bath, try to use colors that are associated with the ritual you have just performed, whether it's through your pajamas, a hair turban, or the sheets you lie in. The energetic power of color will help keep you in your ritual.

✦ ✦ ✦

CREATIVITY BATH

The Creativity Bath can be used whenever you want to bring creativity into any area of your life. You might literally be looking for inspiration or motivation for an artistic project. Or maybe you just want to think through an issue in your life in a more creative way. This bath is particularly effective for those times when you find yourself in a creative rut or when your thoughts are fragmented or difficult to bring into reality.

As you soak in this Creativity Bath, you will feel the citrus soaking into you, energizing both your body and your senses. While we are usually firm believers that less is more, in this case we encourage you to add as much orange as possible because, generally speaking, fruits are very subtle. The more orange you add, the more you will maximize the scent and feel of this bath.

To amplify and add potency to this bath, perform it on a Wednesday, as the energy of that day is most aligned with this intention.

BASE INGREDIENTS

Gold, orange, or silver candle

Basil

Oranges, cut into quarters

Water

HERBS (CHOOSE 1 TO 4)

Bay leaf

Ginger root

Lavender

Rosemary

OILS (CHOOSE 1 TO 4)

Palo santo

Sage

Tangerine

Vanilla

CRYSTALS (CHOOSE 1 STONE)

Black onyx

Citrine

Moldavite

Sodalite

OFFERINGS (CHOOSE 1 TO 5)

Magnet

Magnetic sand

Pumpkin

Silver coins

Yam

SUPPLIES

Lage bowl, for ritual use

Place the candle on your altar and light it as you hold your intention in your mind's eye. Put your offerings on your altar and express gratitude to your ancestors, spirit guides, and the deities that resonate with you.

Remain in a state of intention and prayer as you begin preparing your ingredients. Steep the basil, herbs of your choice, and orange in hot water. Drain the herbs and place them in a bowl, then squeeze the juice of the oranges into the bowl. Add the water, drop in the oil (conservatively for the sake of your plumbing!), and place your crystal in the bowl.

Take the bowl to your altar and infuse it with your intention. You may leave it there for whatever amount of time feels right to you.

When you are ready to take your bath or shower, remove the crystal and place it on your altar. Leave the candle burning as you take the bowl into the bathroom with you. Place the bowl either next

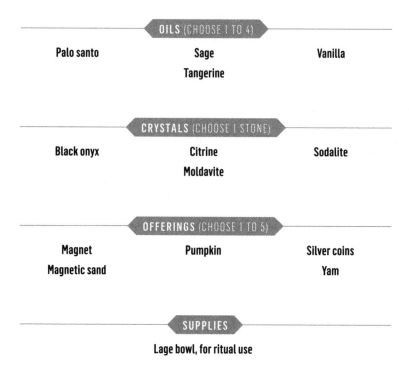

to the tub, or on the floor of the shower if you choose to perform this ritual as a shower.

Ritual baths are generally taken in cooler-temperature water because it's more calming; if you are taking a shower, begin with warm water, then switch to lukewarm or cold when you are ready to actively perform the ritual.

Cleanse your physical body first—use soap, shampoo, and perform all of your normal cleansing practices. Once you have done that, you can turn your attention to your emotional and spiritual bodies. When you are ready to begin the active ritual, hold the bowl above your head and pray, recite your intention, thank your angels, spirit guides, or ancestors, whatever feels right to you. Tilt the bowl and allow the mixture to wash over you. Sweep the mixture over your body, visualizing as you go. As you sweep, you will effectively remove the herbs from your body; this symbolizes removing those things that don't serve you. Visualize all of the things you are washing away—negativity, fear, or any baggage that you might be holding on to unnecessarily. As you let go, you are simultaneously nourishing the new skin that is rising to the surface. As you release, you also receive. Allow yourself to see what you want to activate, or see white light beaming out from around your entire body. Breathe in clarity as you go.

When you are finished, rinse off with water, then towel yourself dry. You may still have some lingering herbs on you, and that's okay. When you dress after your bath, try to use colors that are associated with the ritual you have just performed, whether it's through your pajamas, a hair turban, or the sheets you lie in. The energetic power of color will help keep you in your ritual. (For more on color, see page 111.)

✦ ✦ ✦

ROAD-OPENING BATH

Back in the earliest days of HOI, if we weren't at the store, you could be pretty sure to find us soaking in a Road-Opening Bath. You can still find us there when business is in a slump or we want to open up more options.

This bath will serve all of those same purposes for you. While you're in the bath, you might want to imagine a freeway leading the way to your intention, filled with lots of different exits that represent a variety of options for you to get to your destination.

To amplify and add potency to this bath, perform it on a Monday, as the energy of that day is most aligned with this intention.

BASE INGREDIENTS

Red or orange candle	Pinch of coffee grounds	Water

HERBS (CHOOSE 1 TO 4)

Cinnamon sticks	Salt	Star anise
Lemongrass		

OILS (CHOOSE 1 TO 4)

Citronella	Grapefruit	Mint
	Lemon	

CRYSTALS (CHOOSE 1 STONE)

Fluorite	Lemurian seed quartz	Smoky quartz
	Moss agate	

OFFERINGS (CHOOSE 1 TO 5)

Cigar	Key	Sugar
Dried corn	Rice	

SUPPLIES

Lage bowl, for ritual use

Place the candle on your altar and light it as you hold your intention in your mind's eye. Put your offerings on your altar and express gratitude to your ancestors, spirit guides, and the deities that resonate with you.

Remain in a state of intention and prayer as you begin preparing your ingredients. Steep the coffee grounds and herbs of your choice in hot water. Extract the cinnamon sticks and/or star anise (if you chose to use them), then drain the herbs and place them in a bowl. Add the water, drop in the oil (conservatively for the sake of your plumbing!), and place your crystal in the bowl.

Take the bowl to your altar and infuse it with your intention. You may leave it there for whatever amount of time feels right to you.

When you are ready to take your bath or shower, remove the crystal and place it on your altar. Leave the candle burning as you take the bowl into the bathroom with you. Place the bowl either next to the tub, or on the floor of the shower if you choose to perform this ritual as a shower.

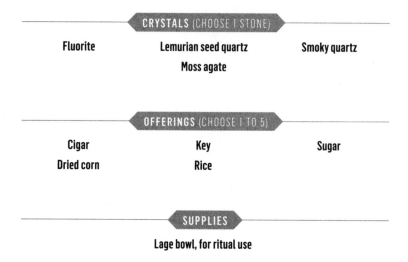

Ritual baths are generally taken in cooler-temperature water because it's more calming; if you are taking a shower, begin with warm water, then switch to lukewarm or cold when you are ready to actively perform the ritual.

Cleanse your physical body first—use soap, shampoo, and perform all of your normal cleansing practices. Once you have done that, you can turn your attention to your emotional and spiritual bodies. When you are ready to begin the active ritual, hold the bowl above your head and pray, recite your intention, thank your angels, spirit guides, or ancestors, whatever feels right to you. Tilt the bowl and allow the mixture to wash over you. Sweep the mixture over your body, visualizing as you go. As you sweep, you will effectively remove the herbs from your body; this symbolizes removing those things that don't serve you. Visualize all of the things you are washing away—negativity, fear, or any baggage that you might be holding on to unnecessarily. As you let go, you are simultaneously nourishing the new skin that is rising to the surface. As you release, you also receive. Allow yourself to see what you want to activate, or see white light beaming out from around your entire body. Breathe in clarity as you go.

When you are finished, rinse off with water, then towel yourself dry. You may still have some lingering herbs on you, and that's okay. When you dress after your bath, try to use colors that are associated with the ritual you have just performed, whether it's through your pajamas, a hair turban, or the sheets you lie in. The energetic power of color will help keep you in your ritual. (For more on color, see page 111.)

✦ ✦ ✦

BATHE IN MONEY AND SUCCESS

When we first started dabbling with magic, we followed rituals as if they were recipes in a cookbook. We were all about precision and accuracy.

Just like people tend to feel more confident freestyling in the kitchen once they have a little experience under their belt, so it was with us and magic. As we became more confident, we began tailoring our magic to our preferences. For example, maybe you've noticed we use a lot of cinnamon in our spells. That's because not only do we love what cinnamon signifies—abundance, money, and love—but we also love how it smells.

You will notice there is cinnamon in this ritual, as there are in so many others. We bet that, as you continue practicing magic, you will develop your own toolkit of go-to ingredients as well.

To amplify and add potency to this bath, perform it on a Thursday, as the energy of that day is most aligned with this intention.

BASE INGREDIENTS

Green, gold, or orange candle

Cinnamon sticks

Rice

Honey

Water

HERBS (CHOOSE 1 TO 4)

Calendula

Parsley

Patchouli

Pine needles

OILS (CHOOSE 1 TO 4)

Allspice	Cinnamon	Peppermint
	Nutmeg	

CRYSTALS (CHOOSE 1 STONE)

Citrine	Lodestone	Tiger's eye
	Pyrite	

OFFERINGS (CHOOSE 1 TO 4)

Almonds	Cowrie shells	Orange
	Grains	

SUPPLIES

Lage bowl, for ritual use

Place the candle on your altar and light it as you hold your intention in your mind's eye. Put your offerings on your altar and express gratitude to your ancestors, spirit guides, and the deities that resonate with you.

Remain in a state of intention and prayer as you begin preparing your ingredients. Steep the cinnamon sticks and herbs of your choice in hot water. Extract the cinnamon sticks, then drain the herbs and place them in a bowl. Add the rice, honey, and water, drop in the oil (conservatively for the sake of your plumbing!), and place your crystal in the bowl.

Take the bowl to your altar and infuse it with your intention. You may leave it there for whatever amount of time feels right to you.

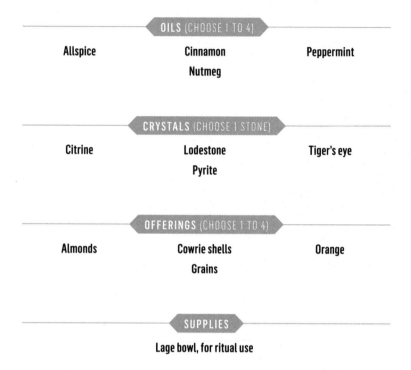

When you are ready to take your bath or shower, remove the crystal and place it on your altar. Leave the candle burning as you take the bowl into the bathroom with you. Place the bowl either next to the tub, or on the floor of the shower if you choose to perform this ritual as a shower.

Ritual baths are generally taken in cooler-temperature water because it's more calming; if you are taking a shower, begin with warm water, then switch to lukewarm or cold when you are ready to actively perform the ritual.

Cleanse your physical body first—use soap, shampoo, and perform all of your normal cleansing practices. Once you have done that, you can turn your attention to your emotional and spiritual bodies. When you are ready to begin the active ritual, hold the bowl above your head and pray, recite your intention, thank your angels, spirit guides, or ancestors, whatever feels right to you. Tilt the bowl and allow the mixture to wash over you. Sweep the mixture over your body, visualizing as you go. As you sweep, you will effectively remove the herbs from your body; this symbolizes removing those things that don't serve you. Visualize all of the things you are washing away—negativity, fear, or any baggage that you might be holding on to unnecessarily. As you let go, you are simultaneously nourishing the new skin that is rising to the surface. As you release, you also receive. Allow yourself to see what you want to activate, or see white light beaming out from around your entire body. Breathe in clarity as you go.

When you are finished, rinse off with water, then towel yourself dry. You may still have some lingering herbs on you, and that's okay. When you dress after your bath, try to use colors that are associated with the ritual you have just performed, whether it's through your pajamas, a hair turban, or the sheets you lie in. The energetic power of color will help keep you in your ritual. (For more on color, see page 111.)

HEALTH & WELLNESS SACHET

The beauty of sachets is that they allow you to carry your ritual out into the real world with you. Also for this reason, we tend to use sachets less frequently than, say, candle magic or ritual baths, precisely because they are *so* powerful and constantly with you. Sachets act as a remembrance of what you want to bring into the world on an ongoing basis as you walk through your life. They provide both physical and emotional strength.

Generally speaking, shells are powerful symbols because they call the ocean home, and the ocean is associated with emotion. You'll notice that this sachet calls for cowrie shells. The reason for this specificity is that cowrie shells are frequently used as a form of divination based on their powerful symbolism. In some traditions, these shells are used as an oracle. Their opening resembles the shape of a mouth; when they face up they represent the angels speaking, when they face down, the angels remain silent. The opening also resembles a vagina, and thus they are a symbol of sacred feminine power.

This particular sachet is great to use during those times when you are experiencing health issues or need to stand strong in the world.

To amplify and maximize the potency of this ritual, perform it on a Sunday, as the energy of that day is best aligned with this intention.

BASE INGREDIENTS

Lavender candle

4 x 9-inch piece of blue or purple cloth

Charm to represent healing (whatever resonates with you; perhaps a cross, deity, dove, saint, etc.)

Cowrie shell

Written list of your health desires

Splash of your personal perfume or Florida Water

Natural cord, such as cotton twine or wool yarn

HERBS (CHOOSE 1 TO 3)

Cinnamon stick

Eucalyptus leaf

5 rose hips

OILS (CHOOSE 1 TO 3)

Frankincense

Lemon

Pine

CRYSTALS (CHOOSE 1 TO 3 STONES)

Aventurine

Bloodstone

Lapis

OFFERINGS

Bread

Coconut

Eggs

Flowers

Light your candle on your altar, place your offerings on your altar, and set your intention.

Place your chosen combination of herbs and oils in a mortar and focus on your intention as you grind them with a pestle (or however else you choose to grind or crush them).

Place the ground herbs in the middle of your piece of cloth. Place your charm, the cowrie shell, and your list of health desires on top of the herb mixture. Spray your perfume or Florida Water over the contents.

Gather the mixture into the center of the cloth and tie the ends together using your natural cord. Place the sachet on your altar to infuse it with your intention and sacred energy. You may choose to leave the sachet on your altar as you continue to focus on that intention, or you might prefer to carry it on you or put it in your purse as a way of bringing energy and intention with you on the go.

When the intention you have set for your sachet feels complete, you can either permanently place the sachet on your altar, extract the crystal, and offer the herbs back to the earth, or dispose of the entire sachet in a garbage can on the grounds of a church or temple, gym, holistic center, or hospital, or in nature.

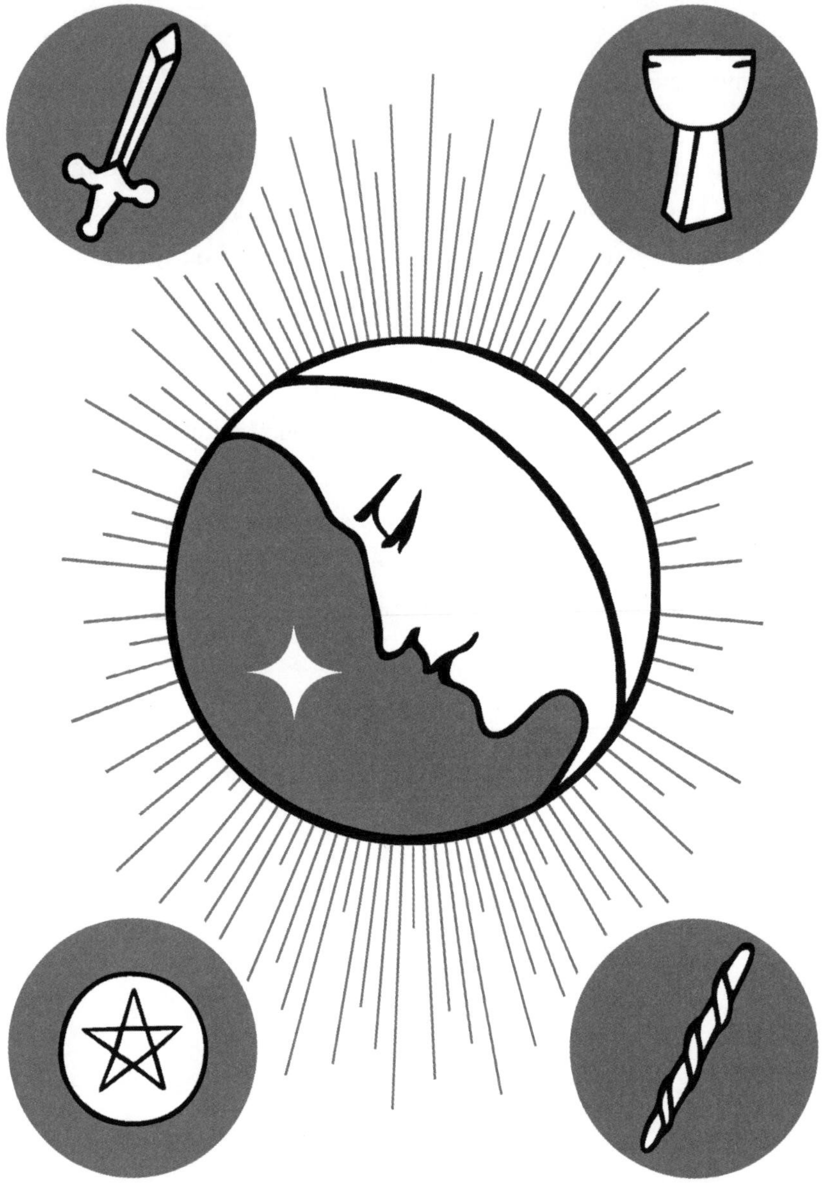

LUCID DREAM SACHET

Do you remember your dreams in all of their detail and vibrancy after you wake up? So many people don't, and that's a shame because messages from your spirit guides and ancestors can come in strongly during your dreams. When you're sleeping, fear and ego drop away. This puts you in a clear state in which it's much easier for spirit to talk to you. However, if you can't vividly remember your dreams, it's hard to make sense of (or even hold on to) these important messages.

This sachet is the perfect solution when you are seeking answers. It's especially good for situations in which you find that your emotions are getting in the way of making decisions. The Lucid Dream Sachet is also a good way of finding clarity during those times when you know you are having a lot of dreams, but can't remember what they're about.

BASE INGREDIENTS

Purple candle

4 x 9-inch piece of purple cloth

Labradorite crystal

Frankincense oil

Natural cord, such as cotton twine or wool yarn

HERBS (CHOOSE 1 TO 5)

Clove

Chamomile

Mugwort

Rosemary

Star anise

Light your candle on your altar, place your offerings on your altar, and set your intention.

Place your chosen combination of herbs in a mortar and focus on your intention as you grind them with a pestle (or however else you choose to grind or crush them).

Place the ground herbs and crystal in the middle of your piece of cloth. If you want, you can include an intention, as well. We like to use this one for our Lucid Dream Sachets: *As I lay my head may I connect with the inner wisdom of my soul. I am hearing and following my divine guidance.* Sprinkle a few drops of the frankincense oil over the contents on the cloth.

Gather the mixture into the center of the cloth and tie the ends together using your natural cord. Place the sachet on your altar to infuse it with your intention and sacred energy. Place the sachet under your pillow and ask the questions you want answers to before going to sleep. Be sure to keep a journal on your nightstand so that you can record the answers you receive when you wake up. It is fascinating to look back over time at the information spirit provides.

When the intention you have set for your sachet feels complete, you can either permanently place the sachet on your altar or extract the crystal and offer the herbs back to the earth.

✦ ✦ ✦

BOX SPELL FOR RELEASING AND LETTING GO

The "box" in box spells represents a coffin for all of the things you don't like about yourself or the situations that aren't working in your life. Because the box symbolizes a coffin, it means that whatever you put inside of it is dead to your experience, never to return. Many people use box spells to let go of people in their life. Understand that this is not done with mal-intent, but as a symbolic representation of reclaiming the space another person holds in your life. This release allows something or someone else to come in.

This ritual sounds easy enough, but people are often surprised by how difficult it is in practice. It's easy enough to say we're done with someone or something, but actually taking action on that is a different thing altogether. It's hard to say goodbye to a way of life or a person once and for all. That's precisely what makes this ritual such an incredibly powerful experience. To get to the point of doing a box ritual, you have to know with your whole heart that you are ready to turn the page to a new chapter.

This ritual goes nicely in tandem with Candle Magic for Heart Healing (see page 193). It is best performed on a Saturday to amplify and maximize the potency of your intention.

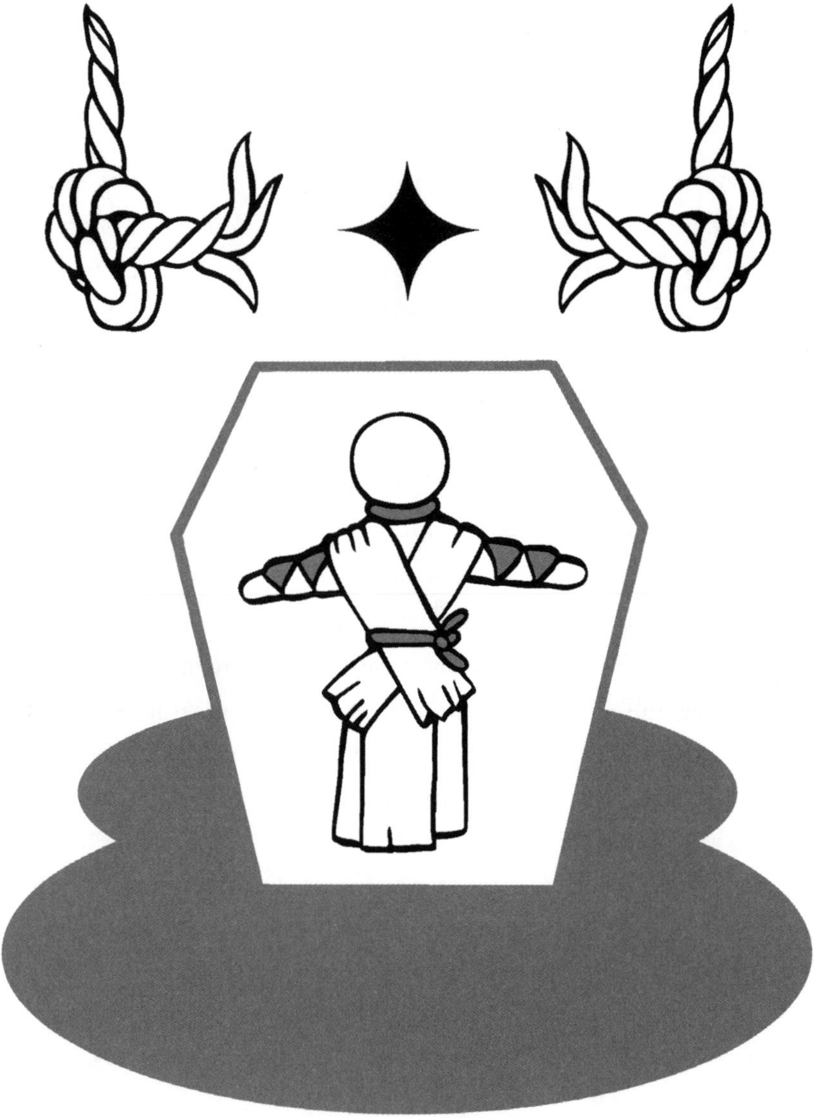

BASE INGREDIENTS

Pinch of black pepper or salt

Lemon peel shavings

Pinch of thyme

Pinch of tobacco from a cigar

Items of your choice that represent the things you would like to release

Small wood box

Poppet (optional, see box page 234)

Paper to write your intention

CRYSTALS (CHOOSE 1 STONE)

Amazonite

Carnelian

Chrysocolla

OFFERINGS (CHOOSE 1 TO 4)

Bread

Coconut

Flowers

Eggs

Place your offering on your altar for your ancestors and set your intention for this box.

In a small bowl, mix together the pepper or salt, lemon peel shavings, thyme, and tobacco. Place the crystal of your choice in with your mixture and set the bowl on your altar.

When you are ready, remove the mixture from your altar. Extract the crystal and sprinkle the mixture along the bottom of your box. Place the items that represent the things you want to release in your box, including the poppet if you so choose. If you would like, write your intention on a piece of paper and include that in your box as well. Seal the box, holding your intention in your mind's eye.

When the ritual feels complete, you may dispose of the box by either burying it or releasing it into the ocean.

✦ ✦ ✦

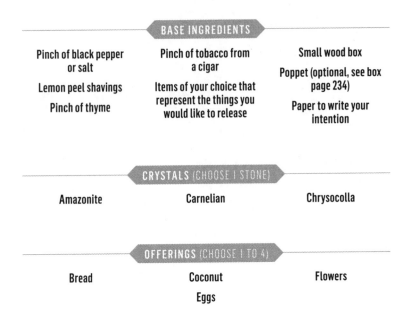

HOW TO MAKE A CLOTH POPPET

Cloth poppets are handmade dolls made of a soft cloth such as cotton or felt, then stuffed with various ingredients. The poppets represent either yourself or someone else. Of course, if your purpose is to help someone else, you must first get their permission to work on their behalf.

Poppets are not voodoo dolls, for one specific reason—how you choose to use them. You can think of it this way: A knife is not a weapon in and of itself. It can be used to cut the food that nourishes your body or it can be used to harm someone. The difference lies in the intention of the person using the knife. Similarly, voodoo dolls are generally used with mal-intent. These poppets are used for good rather than evil, for the health and healing of others and ourselves.

Gather your materials with your intention in mind.

Draw the desired shape of your poppet on a piece of paper or card-stock, then cut it out. Make sure it's big enough that you will have enough room to stuff the figure once you reach that part of the process.

Fold your cloth in half, then trace that shape onto your cloth or cut around it. You should have two cutouts of your desired shape.

Stick the two pieces together.

Turn the material inside out so that the stitches are on the inside. Sew the two pieces of material together, leaving an opening to stuff the poppet.

Stuff your magical blend into the poppet. This might include herbs, oils, coins, or even your intention written on parchment paper and pencil. If it doesn't fill the poppet completely, add in some cotton, wool, straw, or paper, or any objects that signify your intention.

Once stuffed, sew up the opening.

If desired, you can sew on buttons or felt to simulate a face or simply draw a face on.

LUNAR RITUALS

The moon is a great way of amplifying magic, and the rituals associated with the moon's cycles are very simple. The trick is to align your intention with not only the cycle of the moon, but also the sign associated with either the new or full moon.

New moons are a time to usher in the new, to set intentions for things you want to bring into your life. The full moon represents fruition, so it's the time to set intentions that have to do with releasing and letting go. Since new and full moons occur on a monthly basis, lunar rituals are something you can build into your magical routine on a regular basis. We like to amp up this ritual on the first new moon of the year since it is a time of new beginnings. For example, we might create a vision board that aligns with our intentions for the new year and place that on our altar along with the candle. Generally speaking, lunar rituals are a great place to get creative and add your own flair.

Each full and new moon lands in one of the twelve signs, and each sign is associated with specific qualities or areas of life. A simple online search will tell you which sign each new and full moon falls in, and you will want to build your intention around the energy that sign carries (see box on pages 236–7). For example, Capricorn is associated with energies that have to do with work. Whenever possible, it's best to work with the cycles of nature and take advantage of the energy that's being offered to you. That's how you unleash the maximum potency and power of the universe at your disposal!

ZODIAC SIGN
ENERGIES, HERBS & COLORS

✦ ARIES ✦

ENERGY ambition, confidence, dealing with challenges

HERBS black pepper, clove, geranium

COLORS brown, mustard, red, tan

✦ TAURUS ✦

ENERGY devotion, loyalty, patience, slow and steady

HERBS cinnamon, patchouli, rose

COLORS black, brown, dark green, mustard

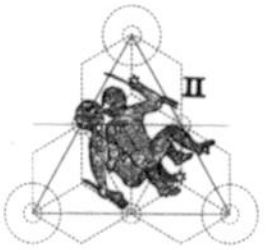

✦ GEMINI ✦

ENERGY adaptable, flexibility, social

HERBS lavender, lemongrass, peppermint

COLORS green (all shades), maroon, yellow

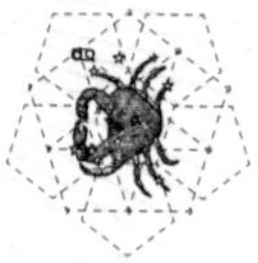

✦ CANCER ✦

ENERGY lunar energy (this is a great sign for moon energy of all types, so any type of intention goes and is fully supported by the universe!)

HERBS chamomile, jasmine, lemon

COLORS light blue, pink, teal, white

✦ LEO ✦

ENERGY beauty, creativity, motivation, self-love

HERBS ginger, mugwort, rosemary

COLORS dark green, red, orange, yellow

✦ VIRGO ✦

ENERGY critical thinking, domination, focus, loyal, organization, passion, perfection

HERBS parsley, patchouli, sage

COLORS dark blue, green (all shades), pink

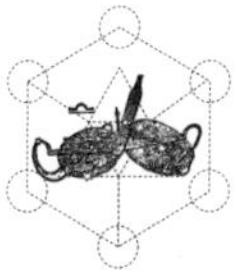

LIBRA

ENERGY	balance, fair-minded, peace-maker, social
HERBS	cinnamon, mugwort, rosemary
COLORS	dark green, pink, red, yellow

SCORPIO

ENERGY	love, passion, strength
HERBS	anise, coffee, pine
COLORS	black, green, red

SAGITTARIUS

ENERGY	enthusiastic, intellectual, optimistic
HERBS	bergamot, nutmeg
COLORS	dark blue, green, purple, yellow

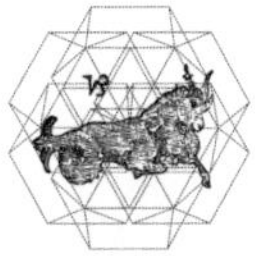

CAPRICORN

ENERGY	business, creativity, stability
HERBS	clove, rosemary, vetivert
COLORS	black, light blue, lavender, purple

AQUARIUS

ENERGY	dreams, insight, unity
HERBS	lavender, patchouli, pine
COLORS	black, light blue, orange, teal

PISCES

ENERGY	compassion, emotions, psychic connections
HERBS	camphor, jasmine, sandlewood
COLORS	light blue, light green, purple, gray

NEW MOON RITUAL

Think of the new moon as your time to plant seeds that you can tend to in order to harvest either a short- or long-term goal. If you're working on something that you would like to bring in before the next new moon arrives, we recommend staying in ritual for the entire month. This doesn't mean you have to do a magic spell for the next thirty days straight—just keep your intention close to the front of your mind as you go about life over the next few weeks.

Ironically (or not), our house astrologer, Chad, found us thanks to a new moon ritual. He had come to Los Angeles to celebrate his friend's birthday, and was planning on staying for a couple of weeks. On the first morning of his visit, Chad and his friends happened to walk into the House of Intuition because they'd been having breakfast nearby. On that visit, Chad bought a crystal and a new moon candle. Something about HOI called to him, so he went back to his friend's house and lit the candle for the new moon in Libra that night. He set an intention to get a job at HOI.

Before the full moon came around, the job was his and Chad's plans to spend just a couple of weeks in L.A. went out the window.

Chad's example points to something interesting. Chad set a career-focused intention while the new moon was in Libra, despite the fact that Libra is not a career-oriented sign. Because Chad is an astrologer, though, he understood that Libra was situated in the north node of his chart, which is all about destiny and strategy—as was his intention.

This illustrates how expansive new moon rituals can be. Beginners can align their intentions with basic information about the signs (as provided in the Zodiac Energies box), while those with a more advanced understanding of astrology can dig deeper into how the sign in which the new moon is stationed correlates with their personal birth chart. Of course, most important of all is the fact that the new moon represents the time for starting new cycles.

Also important and worth noting is that Chad followed his intuition, even if it didn't make a lot of sense—after all, he knew nothing about HOI prior to this visit, and he wasn't planning on staying in L.A. But he listened to his intuition when it spoke up, and worked in accordance with the cycles of the universe. Because of this, he ended up walking down an entirely new path that turned out to be perfectly suited for him.

And, finally, a pro tip: Journaling is a great tool for new moon rituals because the practice allows you to look back to see your daily thoughts, your journey, and to keep a written record of any messages you might receive from spirit.

INGREDIENTS

Candle, with the color associated with the sign the new moon lands in

Herbs and/or oils associated with the sign of the new moon

SUPPLIES

Pen

Piece of brown paper or parchment paper

Journal (optional)

Holding your intention in mind, clean the candle with water and a cloth, trim the wick, and anoint the candle with herbs or oils that amplify the sign the moon is in. Rub the oils and herbs clockwise around the top of the candle to draw your intention toward you. When you are finished, place your candle on your altar.

Write your intention down on the piece of paper, place the paper under the candle, and light your candle.

Since new moon cycles happen so frequently and often involve short-term goals, we like to hold on to our written intentions over time so that we can look back on them and recognize the universe at work.

✦ ✦ ✦

FULL MOON RITUAL

During the full moon, call to mind those things you need to release. What is weighing you down? What habits, people, or circumstances are not conducive to your highest good? Now is the time to let it go.

INGREDIENTS

- Candle, with the color associated with the sign the full moon lands in
- Herbs and/or oils associated with the sign of the full moon

SUPPLIES

- Pen
- Piece of brown paper or parchment paper
- Journal (optional)

With those things you need to release in mind, clean the candle with water and a cloth, trim the wick, and then anoint the candle with herbs or oils that amplify the sign the moon is in. Rub the oils and herbs counterclockwise around the top of the candle to release those things in your life that you are ready to let go of. When you are finished, place your candle on your altar.

On your piece of paper, write down everything that you are ready to let go of. Light your candle as you ask your guides, ancestors, the universe, and your highest self to assist you in releasing all of the things on this piece of paper as well as anything else that may not be serving you. Carefully burn the peace of paper with your candle.

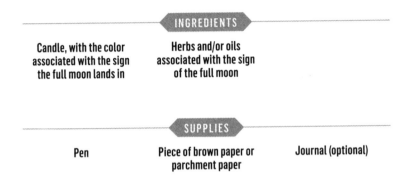

After we have completed this ritual, we generally like to pour some salt into a bath and soak to amplify the moon's cleansing and clearing energies. Other things you might want to do as part of your full moon ritual are rearranging your furniture or cleaning out your closet and donating those things you have not worn or used in the past 6 months. Both of these help to move and uplift the energy in your space and release attachment to the past.

✦ ✦ ✦

SUN RITUAL

Today, more and more people are aware of the cycles of the moon and how they can be utilized in a personal magic or spiritual practice. What people don't talk about as much are sun rituals.

There are few things more important to human survival than the sun. And yet, so often we take it for granted. Historically, though, the sun has been worshipped across cultures as the provider of light, warmth, and, most important, the source of life.

As you'll see, sun rituals are very simple; they're also very rewarding. This ritual is meant to be performed as the sun breaks over the horizon. It's a great way to start your day on either an occasional or regular basis.

INGREDIENT

1 stick frankincense incense

Prepare your sacred space by burning your stick of frankincense. Position yourself comfortably, either sitting or standing, and facing east so that you can watch as the sun rises.

As the sun begins to rise, gaze at the beautiful colors cast across the horizon. Hold your intention for your day in mind as you witness nature's beauty. Visualize your intention as a seed, and see the sun's light giving life to your intention and growing it into fruition. As the sun rises higher and its warmth begins to radiate over you, release

any stress or anxiety you may be holding into the golden sheen of the sun.

When your ritual feels complete, reach your arms up and out toward the sun as if you were hugging it. Give thanks to the sun for providing another day full of opportunities to be the best version of yourself.

✦ ✦ ✦

APPENDIX

CRYSTALS

AMAZONITE ✦ calms the mind, confident expression, empowerment, removes blockages, self-discovery, soothes trauma

AMETHYST ✦ higher consciousness, lucid dreaming, psychic protection, purifies, removes clutter, stone of sobriety

APACHE TEARS ✦ empathetic stone, heals energetic scarring, protects and supports during times of deep grief and loss

AVENTURINE ✦ abundance, lucky stone, prosperity, stimulates metabolism, "winning" vibration

BERYL ✦ focus on the bigger picture, helps to deal with daily stressors, inspires optimism

BLACK OBSIDIAN ✦ deflects negative energy, grounding, projects visions and messages, psychic protection, shields

BLACK ONYX ✦ grounds, offers guidance, perseverance, strength, transmutes negativity into positivity

BLACK TOURMALINE ✦ absorbs and dispels negative energy, grounds, ultimate protector

BLOODSTONE ✦ assertion of boundaries, earth energy for health, heals the blood, helps with blood family relationships, inspires confidence, purifies and detoxifies the body

BLUE APATITE ✦ ambition, clears the mind, communication, intuitive awareness, personal power, stimulates motivation

CARNELIAN ✦ courage, creativity, heals childhood trauma, vitality

CHRYSOCOLLA ✦ divine feminine, heals heart trauma, promotes inner strength, sparks knowledge through experience, wisdom

CHRYSOPRASE ✦ heals inner child trauma, reconnects to the heart, reflection, releases egotistical perspectives

CITRINE ✦ abundance, creativity, imagination, magnetism, manifesting stone, money, motivation, success

CLEAR QUARTZ ✦ aids in concentration, enhances psychic abilities, helps manifesting, master healer, raises the vibration in a space

FLUORITE ✦ absorbs negative energy, cleanses aura and chakras, clears the mind of clutter, enhances mental function, shields from psychic manipulation

GARNET ✦ abundance, detoxification, love, luck, removes energetic blockages

GREEN CALCITE ✦ absorbs pain and toxicity, great companion for house plants, healer of the heart, helps remove anxieties and fears, ignites inner fire

JADE + balance, good luck, harmony, heals the heart, helps connect the body with the spirit, purity, serenity

KUNZITE + connection to divine love, heart opening, higher consciousness, purity, unconditional love, wisdom

LABRADORITE + dream recall, helps harness psychic abilities, spiritual growth, strengthens intuition, strengthens the will

LAPIS + abundance, assists with organization, cleanses and purifies the body, communication, decision making, willpower

LEMURIAN SEED QUARTZ + awakens higher and intra-dimensional consciousness, clarity, grows a dream or plan, offers spiritual healing, removes blockages

LODESTONE + attraction, clears thoughts, focuses, grounds, polarizes by balancing male and female energy, stone of magnetism

MOLDAVITE + astral travel, extraterrestrial energy, intense transformative energy, removes blocks, spiritual awakening

MOONSTONE + connects to the moon and divine feminine, happiness, introspection, mothering, nurturing, selflessness

MOSS AGATE + confidence, creativity, heals, new beginnings, ushers in growth of new ideas

PYRITE + abundance, attracts good luck, grounds, manifesting stone, promotes luck, prosperity, protects, warrior shield

ROSE QUARTZ + helps clear anger, resentment, and jealousy; matters of the heart; nurtures; strengthens bonds; unconditional love

RUBY + devotion, motivates, passion, promotes wealth and well-being, vitality

SELENITE + brings in divine white light, cleanses, higher wisdom, peace, removes negativity and energy blocks

SHUNGITE + antioxidant, balances the energy of conflict, brings harmony, detoxifies, grounds, removes negativity

SMOKY QUARTZ + brings in emotional calmness, grounds, maintains focus on goals, relieves stress and anxiety, protects, soothes

SODALITE + brings order and calmness, brings us back to center, harmony, heightens intuition, self-acceptance, self-esteem, trust

TIGER'S EYE + balances, clarity, concentration, courage, fierceness, harmony, intense focus, power, promotes positive thoughts and action, strength

TURQUOISE + abundance, clarity, master healer, power, protection against negativity, tranquility, wisdom

FLOWERS, FOODS, AND GOODS

ALOE PLANT ✦ luck, protects, spiritual growth, shields against evil

APPLE ✦ love, luck, removes enemies

AVOCADO ✦ beauty, heals, love, youth

BEER ✦ detoxifies, protects from the evil eye, removes negativity

BLACK SALT ✦ creates an energetic boundary, expels negativity, removes someone or something from your space or self

BREAD ✦ body of life, eternal life, offering of gratitude

CANDY ✦ celebration, happiness, sweetens up a space

CARNATIONS (WHITE) ✦ luck, offering to the spirit world, pure love, purifies

CHAMPAGNE ✦ celebration, enjoyment, excitement, happiness, love

CHERRY ✦ clarity, happiness, love, passion, romance

CINNAMON ✦ abundance, fast movement, love, promotes dreaming, protection, spiritual growth, success, wealth

COCONUT ✦ cleanses, prosperity, protects, purifies, success

COFFEE ✦ assists in removing negative thoughts, dispels nightmares, grounds, overcomes internal blocks, peace of mind, reverses witchcraft, speeds up spells

CORN ✦ abundance, good luck, protects

EGGS ✦ cleanses, purification

EUCALYPTUS LEAF ✦ cleanses, fast healing, health, protects, purifies

FLOWERS ✦ offering to the spirits

GARLIC ✦ exorcism, home and business blessing, inner strength, protection

HONEY ✦ abundance, attraction, beauty, financial gain, love

JASMINE ✦ aphrodisiac, dreams, feminine power, love, sex, spiritual growth

LEMON ✦ clears the mind, enhances awareness, heals, psychic power, uplifts

MILK ✦ cleanses, calms, nurtures, purifies

ORANGE ✦ calm, happiness, luck, peace

PAPAYA ✦ intensifies love, keeps evil away, reverses hexes and jinxes

PUMPKIN ✦ fertility, grants wishes, love, protection, purity

RICE ✦ absorbs negativity, abundance, blessings, foundation of life, harvest

ROSE (RED) ✦ heals, love, luck, passion, romance

ROSE (WHITE) ✦ innocence, long-lasting love, new beginnings, purifies

SAGE ✦ blessings, cleanses, heals, knowledge, protection, purifies, sacred, wisdom

SALT ✦ banishes negativity, cleanses, removes, represents the emotional body

STAR ANISE ✦ dreams, protects, sleep, spiritual growth

SUGAR ✦ attracts sweetness

SUNFLOWER ✦ assists with grief, connects to angelic beings and the faerie realm, fertility, love, loyalty, uplifts spirit

TOBACCO ✦ banishes, heals, offering of gratitude to the gods, purifies, summons and dominates spirits

VINEGAR ✦ protects, rids enemies and unwanted energy, wards off evil spirits

VODKA ✦ blows fire, burns away energy, courage, motivates, strength

WATER ✦ cleanses, renews, purifies

YAMS ✦ encourages friendship, grounds, harmony, nurtures

HERBS AND OILS

ALLSPICE ✦ money, prosperity, protects from poverty, success

BASIL ✦ business and general blessings, cleanses, divination, prosperity, protects, wards off negative energy

BAY LEAF ✦ divination, heals, money, protection, strength, success

BERGAMOT ✦ clarity of mind, fertility, happiness, physical energy, prosperity, sleep, success

CALENDULA ✦ happiness, protects, spiritual growth

CAMPHOR ✦ cleanses the aura, dispels fear and lower-vibration negative energy, helps alleviate stress, protects and shields

CHAMOMILE ✦ attracts money, calms, cleanses, heals, meditation, peace, sleep

CINNAMON ✦ abundance, love, promotes dreaming, protection, spiritual growth, success, wealth

CITRONELLA ✦ clears evil, helps with depression, protects, uplifts the spirit

CLOVE ✦ activates other ingredients, clarity, protects

CYPRESS ✦ blessings, comfort, happiness, harmony, heals, inspires, peace

EUCALYPTUS ✦ balance, cleanses, health, heals, purifies

FRANKINCENSE ✦ accelerates spiritual growth, blessings, cleanses, heals, protects, purifies

GARLIC ✦ exorcises, inner strength

GERANIUM ✦ assurance, balance, confidence, feminine energy, heals, love, meditation, protects, tranquility

GINGER ROOT ✦ amplifies spells, courage, love, luck, prosperity, protects, sexuality

GRAPEFRUIT ✦ awakens, energizes, increases mental clarity, promotes feelings of love and opens one up to emotions, revitalizes

LAVENDER ✦ balances chakras, calms, cleanses, good for sleep, happiness, heals, love, maintains health, peace, purifies, relaxes, tranquility

LEMON ✦ cleanses, clears, cuts, maintains good health, purifies, rejuvenates, removes

LEMONGRASS ✦ clears the path, love, mental clarity, psychic powers, spiritual growth

LIME ✦ heals, love, physical energy, protects, purifies

MANDARIN ✦ alleviates grief and loneliness, awakens the spirit, calms, connects to your inner child, inspires, soothes, uplifts

MINT ✦ cuts and breaks away negativity, heals, prosperity, protects, safe travels

MUGWORT ✦ connects with the spirit world and ancestors, divination, heals, inner strength, lucid dreaming

MYRRH ✦ cleanses, grounds, heals, spirituality, trauma healing, peace, purifies

NUTMEG ✦ clarity of mind, luck, prosperity, protection

ORANGE ✦ conquers fears and obsessions, creativity, divination, happiness of the heart, joy, positivity

OREGANO ✦ happiness, heals, love, prosperity, tranquility

PALO SANTO ✦ cleanses, creates a sacred space, lifts the vibration of a space, purifies, removes negativity

PARSLEY ✦ luck, healing, purifies, protects

PATCHOULI ✦ connects with the spirit realm, love, removes hexes, passion, prosperity, seduction

PEPPER ✦ banishes negativity, courage, physical energy, protects

PEPPERMINT ✦ calms, clarifies the mind, dreams, sharpens focus, ushers in financial gain

PINE ✦ enhances focus on your direction, fertility, good health, heals, humility, mindfulness, money, prosperity, success

ROSE HIPS ✦ heals, health, invokes spirit, love

ROSEMARY ✦ heals, mental clarity, peace, psychic powers, protects

SAGE ✦ cleanses, knowledge, purifies, wisdom

SANDALWOOD ✦ calms and uplifts energy, meditation, protects

STAR ANISE ✦ boosts psychic awareness and spells, brings good luck, promotes dreams, spiritual growth and protection

TANGERINE ✦ awakens joy, dissolves negativity, energizes, strength

THYME ✦ balance, calming, courage, heals, promotes restful sleep, spiritual growth, stops nightmares

VANILLA ✦ love, loyalty, mental power, money, seduction

WHITE COPAL ✦ brings in higher-vibration energy, connects to the spirit realm, creates a sacred space, protects, purifies

YLANG-YLANG ✦ brings peace to situations, happiness, inner calm, love, tranquility

ACKNOWLEDGMENTS

THANK YOU FROM MARLENE

To all of our following and supporters—to every single person who has walked into our stores, followed our social pages, browsed our online store, or taken a class with us—thank you for so many years of trust and allowing us to be part of your spiritual journey. We are so grateful to walk this path with you. Because of all of you, House of Intuition has been our dream come true.

Marc Gerald, thank you for seeing a vision for a book we did not see for ourselves, and for your persistence in helping us see it, too. Your guidance and love throughout the process have been invaluable. You are more than our agent; you are a friend for life!

Nikki Van Noy, you are a true gift from our spirits! Throughout this project you calmed our nerves and made us laugh, while guiding us down memory lane. It has been such a pleasure to work with you.

Donna Loffredo, thank you for seeing our vision and believing in us, for being so gentle and guiding us with your expertise. You were the perfect fit for us. And to the entire team at Penguin Random House: we are so blessed to have been able to work with such a kind team of amazing professionals. Your encouragement gave us the strength and confidence we needed to deliver a book we are so proud of.

Valentina Zapata, thank you for your ten-plus years of support and for always being willing to help us create a magical space through your gift of artistry. Every stroke of your paint brush has made each of our stores and the pages of our book feel as if they were blessed by Heaven above. Love you, Val.

To the HOI team past, present, and future: thanks to each one of you for making our dreams come true, and for your support and belief in our mission. We are forever grateful. A special thank you to Carol, Ryan, Chad, and Jaakko for your testimonials.

Kathy, thank you for taking me to my first tarot card reading and for showing me that it's okay to explore and experience things for myself before placing judgement on a spiritual practice. You were the beginning of my spiritual awakening and I love you for showing me a world I did not know existed.

Marcy, thank you for taking this journey with me, for being my soul sister in this lifetime and beyond, and for giving me the ability to love unconditionally. I am so proud to have my big sister by my side and for all of your hard work. I love you more than I can ever express on a human level.

Daddy, you have given me the gift of dreaming big and believing that anything is possible. Your love has carried my entrepreneurship to levels I never knew were possible. You are the King in my life. Thank you for loving me the way you do and being the best father I could ever ask for. I love you and will always be a daddy's girl.

Momma, thank you for showing me how to be a strong woman and the meaning of a good work ethic. I'm so grateful for the many hours you've spent filling our incense bags and tins and oil bottles, and helping us however else we've needed. I know you are always there and willing to give a hand. I love you, my Queen.

Auntie Ruthie, thank you for your many visits and the blessings you bestow upon me daily. Your spirit has been my saving grace in so many ways. I miss your physical being and contagious laugh, but I know your spirit body will always be with me. I love you, my guardian angel.

Eric, thank you, son, for always being so understanding and supportive of my dreams. You give me the motivation to always be a better version of myself. For all the days and long nights when I worked endlessly, your understanding and love have never wavered. I love you, baby boy!

Alex, thank you for being my rock, for always standing by my side and allowing me to spread my wings in the world in a way I never knew was possible. You are my best friend, my partner, and the love of my life. I thank God every day for you, my little lucky charm! I love you from the top of your head to the tip of your toes. Forever and ever!

THANK YOU FROM ALEX

Writing this book was much harder than I could have ever imagined because I am a very private person. On the flip side, it was also very rewarding to be able to talk about my life journey and the many experiences that have brought me to where I am today. None of this would have been possible without some very special people who have crossed my path. First and foremost, I'd like to thank God and all my spirit guides for always having my back.

Marc, thank you for stalking us (lol) and not taking no for an answer. You believed in our mission and your support and encouragement really helped the process. If it wasn't for your relentless perseverance, we would not be writing this book.

Nikki, I can't thank you enough for your openness and ability to capture our personalities during our storytelling times. You really made this process so much fun and truly therapeutic. You are the perfect fit for us and I look forward to working with you again.

Donna, thank you for your guidance while always giving us the freedom to express ourselves freely. You have really made this process such a pleasure and not as intimidating.

To everyone we worked with at Penguin Random House, I could not be more thankful and happy for having you all be a part of this journey. I'm truly grateful and I feel we made the best choice for such an important milestone in our journey.

Valentina, oh my little Valentina, thank you for always being there for us and sharing your amazing talents. It's been such a pleasure having you on this journey with us on both a professional and personal level. You're an amazing artist and an even better human. I look forward to many more years of collaborations with you.

Tia Nena, you were ripped from my life way too soon, however I know that you have always been up in heaven watching over me as you did when you were here. Thank you for the messages and for always ensuring that I feel I have a guardian angel that is always with me, protecting and guiding me. Until we meet again, I love you dearly!

Mami, thank you for always being there for me and our family. You are one of the strongest women I have ever met. Thank you for teaching me and giving me a spiritual foundation and allowing me to explore and find my way without judgement. I'm also thankful for your willingness to always help us in the potion room—you are the best candle cleaner ever! I love you endlessly, Mami!

Papi, thank you for accepting me, never judging me, and listening to me whenever I need a shoulder to cry on. I admire your ability to stay positive in the most difficult moments and to see the cup half full rather than half empty. I love you endlessly, Papi!

Thank you to my little brother Marvin, for loving and supporting me in the purest form. Your carefree personality is admirable, but also really gets on my nerves sometimes (lol). I love you endlessly, bruh!

HOI family, thank you to every single person that is, has been, and will be part of this entity that is so much bigger than all of us. Thank you for being a part of a collective striving to spread knowledge, love, light, and self-empowerment.

Eric, thank you for your love and support when we came to you to borrow your college education money to help us start HOI and for being so understanding when we were caught up working 12- to 14-hour days at the store. Thank you for accepting me into your and your mother's life journey and for being part of my journey. I love you, Nelson.

Marlene, you have been my rock and, without you, this would not be possible. You have taught me so much and brought out the best in me. I truly believe outside forces brought us together and I thank God, our spirits, and the universe for such divine intervention. I love you to the moon and back!

INDEX

Note: Page numbers in *italics* indicate rituals and ritual ingredients. Page numbers in **bold** indicate summaries of items' influences.

ABOUT THE AUTHORS

Alex Naranjo and **Marlene Vargas** are the founders of House of Intuition, which has grown from a small shop offering crystals, tarot, and intuitive services to one of the largest, well-known metaphysical brands in the US. Currently, there are numerous store locations sprinkled throughout California and Florida, with plans for more on the horizon. In addition to handcrafting an array of ritual tools such as intention candles and oils, House of Intuition offers a cosmic classroom of esoteric subjects, metaphysical services, and Hoi.tv, a digital platform focused on sharing knowledge of spiritual practices that bring healing, perspective, and magic.